THE

HBCU

EXPERIENCE

THE NORTH CAROLINA A&T STATE UNIVERSITY
3rd EDITION

Visionary Author: Dr. Ashley Little
President Letter: Chancellor Harold L. Martin Sr., Ph.D.
Foreword Author: Dr. Judy Rashid

For permission requests, write to the publisher, addressed|

"Attention Permissions Coordinator," at
thehbcuexperiencemovement@gmail.com

Published By: The HBCU Experience Movement, LLC

The HBCU Experience Movement, LLC

thehbcuexperiencemovement@gmail.com

Ordering Information:
Quantity Sales: Special discounts are available on quantity purchases by corporations, associations, and nonprofits. For details, contact the publisher at the address above.

Photo Credit: Dr. Stephen Jarrelle Harris
Photo Credit: Desmond L. Kemp

ISBN: 978-1-7349311-9-8

CHANCELLOR HAROLD L. MARTIN SR., PH.D.

A Message from the Chancellor
Harold L. Martin Sr., Ph.D.

I was 8 1/2 years old, growing up in Winston-Salem, when the A&T Four electrified the nation with their legendary sit-in at the downtown Greensboro Woolworth.

Television networks, magazines and radio news covered the demonstration led by four North Carolina A&T freshmen as it played out over six months. At its end, not only Woolworth but other public retail and dining establishments had integrated or were taking steps toward integration. The A&T Four and other A&T, Bennett College and Dudley High students who took part in the sit ins at Woolworth and other eateries created a righteous, real-world illustration of the plain need for changes in federal and state law banning racial discrimination in businesses serving the public.

Certainly, I had an idea of what a university was before that auspicious day in 1960 when those four young men sat down. But this was more than whatever I had imagined until that point. The A&T Four planted an important seed of understanding within me that a university could be a place where people interested in making things better come together. Working together, they could be a powerful force for change.

My older brother and sister chose A&T. When it came my time a couple years later, I followed, enrolling for my freshman year not quite three months after the 1969 Greensboro Uprising drew hundreds of U.S. troops to the A&T campus. One young man, Willie Grimes, lost his life in gunfire during that siege, which 61 years later remains the largest mobilization of U.S. military in our nation's history on a college campus.

It was a sobering moment, but it didn't dampen my enthusiasm for A&T at all. To the contrary, A&T continued to be to me a place where the status quo was no longer acceptable, a place that wouldn't turn a blind eye to the kind of institutional injustice that drove the protests leading to the uprising. I dove into its academic deep end and swam as hard as I could.

I had originally intended to play basketball for A&T. I quickly came to understand that I could either succeed as an engineering student or play basketball, but I couldn't do both well. It was a tough decision, but with my concentration fully on my studies, I earned a B.S. in Electrical Engineering, and a master's degree immediately following that.

A&T did not yet offer doctoral degrees at that time, and I opted to earn my Ph.D. at Virginia Tech, where I experienced life in higher education beyond the campus boundaries of an HBCU – a predominantly white land grant created about 20 years before A&T. Evidence of differences in the ways that state governments treat PWI and HBCU land grants was all around me. I took that knowledge and those memories with me when I earned my Ph.D. and returned to A&T as a newly minted faculty member.

I moved up the ranks to department chair, dean of engineering and vice chancellor for Academic Affairs before accepting my first chancellorship at Winston-Salem State University, and then the executive vice presidency of Academic Affairs for the UNC System. In 2009, I accepted the chancellorship of A&T, returning to become its first alumnus chancellor. Today, I am surrounded by an incredibly capable leadership team an outstanding faculty and tremendous students. Indeed, as I first understood many years before, they have become a powerful force for change, not just on our campus but in higher education.

All but nine of my 41 years as an academic professional have been spent in this incredible place. Other places have beckoned, some with big names or weighty reputations. But as the poet Robert Frost said, where "two roads diverged … I took the one less traveled by, and that has made all the difference."

I have had the privilege of watching A&T emerge as a true national leader – in STEM education, as the nation's top producer of Black graduates in a wide range of disciplines and as a high-achieving research institution routinely collaborating with the nation's best-known science campuses. Today's entering student has an average GPA of 3.7 and an SAT score approaching 1,100, and our enrollment goal of 14,000 by 2023 – once thought to be a stretch – is now well within our grasp.

Just as importantly, our graduate programs are rapidly evolving. This fall, we set a new enrollment record of 1,726 graduate students in masters and doctoral programs and in post-doc initiatives. As our size grows and our quality deepens, we see no stopping point for our evolution and maturation as a university – only bigger hills to climb.

It's certainly a far cry from 131 years ago, when a brave group of trailblazers established A&T's forerunner in a small annex of Shaw University, or from 130 years ago, when those same leaders made the decision to build our home in Greensboro. With 14 acres of donated land and $11,000 in cash – incredibly modest resources by any measure – they laid the groundwork for the university I was privileged to attend and am blessed to serve to this day.

And while they laid the groundwork, the A&T Four lit the path that led me here, as they did for so many others. I will forever be grateful for that, and for the opportunity to lead this amazing university for going on 13 years. It is a beacon of hope and possibility whose brightness has only increased over time.

May it shine brightly for the next generation, the one after that, and the endless march of humanity that I hope will forever look to A&T for the righteous way forward.

About Chancellor Harold L. Martin Sr., Ph.D.

Harold Lee Martin Sr., Ph.D., was elected the 12th chancellor of North Carolina Agricultural and Technical State University on May 22, 2009, and formally began his tenure on June 8, 2009. Martin brought more than 30 years of transformative leadership experience in higher education to the role. He is the first alumnus to serve as the university's chief executive.

Martin's leadership has been distinguished by a focus on long-range strategic planning and tactical leadership that have dramatically improved North Carolina A&T's standing among the nation's land grant, doctoral research universities, as well as among historically Black colleges and universities (HBCU). The initial strategic plan implemented under Martin's direction, "A&T Preeminence 2020: Embracing Our Past, Creating Our Future," saw A&T expand research contract and grant funding, boost its status as one of North Carolina's top three public research institutions, reorganize its colleges and academic programs, increase endowment holdings by 150% and become the nation's largest HBCU. Having surpassed numerous goals in that plan three years ahead of schedule, Martin introduced a refreshed plan in 2018, "A&T Preeminence: Taking the Momentum to 2023," which creates bold new aspirations in student success, affordability, enrollment, research, diversity and more. More than ever, the university's planning under Martin's management sets it on a course for making a significant difference in the lives of its constituents and the communities they serve.

An institution recognized for its leadership in science, technology, engineering and mathematics (STEM), N.C. A&T has expanded its focus on academic excellence to include all disciplines. Under Martin's leadership, it has become one of the nation's top producers of African American graduates in engineering, mathematics, statistics, agriculture, journalism, visual and performing arts, marketing and physical sciences. In 2015, the university earned the Community Engagement Classification by the Carnegie Foundation for the Advancement of Teaching. During Martin's tenure, the university has continually increased student enrollment (now 12,754) while sustaining quality students and has grown its statewide economic impact to more than $1.5 billion.

Martin has also been instrumental in establishing and fostering strategic partnerships such as the Joint School of Nanoscience and Nanoengineering at the Gateway University Research Park (South Campus) and playing a significant role in Opportunity Greensboro, the city's alliance between the seven colleges and universities and the business community that is intended to make Greensboro a national model for collaboration in knowledge-based economic development.

Before his election as chancellor of A&T, Martin served as senior vice president for academic affairs for the UNC System. He also served as the 11th chief administrator and seventh chancellor of Winston-Salem State University and in a number of administrative posts at A&T including vice chancellor for the Division of Academic Affairs, dean of the College of Engineering and chairman of the Department of Electrical Engineering.

A proponent of community engagement, Martin lends himself to service on various boards including the American Council on Education, the Association of Public and Land-Grant Universities, Southern Association of Colleges and Schools Review Advisory Board, Research Triangle Institute, Piedmont Triad Regional Development Council, National Collegiate Athletic Association Limited-Resource Institutions Advisory Group.

Martin was heralded as an education and business thought leader in TIME magazine's August 2020 edition of The Leadership Brief. In 2019, he was honored by the Thurgood Marshall College Fund with the Education Leadership Award, and in 2017 he was named

America's most influential HBCU leader by HBCU Digest, which came on the heels of him being named one of the Triad Business Journal's 2016 Most Admired CEOs. In 2015, Martin was named to the EBONY Power 100 list alongside some of the nation's most prominent African American thinkers, artists, government officials and business leaders.

The Winston-Salem, N.C., native received his B.S. and M.S. degrees in electrical engineering from A&T and a Ph.D. in electrical engineering from Virginia Polytechnic Institute and State University. He is a member of Tau Beta Pi (The Engineering Honor Society), Eta Kappa Nu Association, The Honor Society of Phi Kappa Phi, Beta Gamma Sigma and Alpha Phi Alpha Fraternity Inc.

Martin and his wife Davida, the former county attorney for Forsyth County, North Carolina, have two adult sons and three grandchildren.

DR. ASHLEY LITTLE

A Message from the Founder
Dr. Ashley Little

Historically Black Colleges & Universities (HBCUs) were established to serve the educational needs of black Americans. During the time of their establishment, and many years afterward, blacks were generally denied admission to traditionally white institutions. Prior to The Civil War, there was no structured higher education system for black students. Public policy, and certain statutory provisions, prohibited the education of blacks in various parts of the nation. Today, HBCUs represent a vital component of American higher education.

The HBCU Experience Movement, LLC is a collection of stories from prominent alumni throughout the world, who share how their HBCU experience molded them into the people they are today. We are also investing financially into HBCUs throughout the country. Our goal is to create a global movement of prominent HBCU alumni throughout the nation to continue to share their stories each year, allowing us to give back to prestigious HBCUs annually.

We are proud to present to you *The HBCU Experience: The North Carolina A&T State University 3rd Edition*. We would like to give special thanks to Chancellor Harold L. Martin Sr., Ph.D. thank you for believing in the movement and all you continue to do for North Carolina Agricultural & Technical State University. Next, we would like to give special thanks to our amazing Foreword Author Dr. Judy Rashid and our TrailBlazer Royall M. Mack, Sr. We would like to acknowledge and give special thanks to our Contributing Authors and Official Partners of North Carolina A&T State University for believing in this movement and investing your time, and monetary donations, to give back to your school. Thank you all for your hard

work and dedication on behalf of this project. We appreciate all of
the Notable Aggie Alumni who shared your HBCU experience in
this publication. Aggie Pride!!!!

About Dr. Ashley Little

Dr. Ashley Little is The CEO/Founder of Ashley Little Enterprises, LLC which encompasses her Media, Consulting Work, Writing, Ghost Writing, Book Publishing, Book Coaching, Project Management, Magazine, Public Relations & Marketing, and Empowerment Speaking. In addition, she is an Award-Winning Serial Entrepreneur, TV/Radio Host, TEDx Speaker, International Speaker, Keynote Speaker, Media Maven, Journalist, Writer, Host, Philanthropist, Business Coach, Investor, Advisor for She Wins Society and 15X Award-Winning Best Selling Author. As seen on Black Enterprise(2X), Sheen Magazine (Print and Online), Sheen Talk, Voyage ATL, Fox Soul TV, NBC, Fox, CBS, BlackNews.Com, Shoutout Miami, Shoutout Atlanta, TEDx Speaker, Morning Star, Yahoo Finance, Heart and Soul, The Book of Sean, HBCU Times, VIP Global Magazine, The Black Report, Vocal, Ted.com, Medium, Soul Wealth, Hustle and Soul, BlackBusiness.com, New York Weekly Top 10 Hardest Working CEOs alongside Billionaire Mark Cuban, US Insiders Top 10 Women Entrepreneurs alongside Billionaire and Media Mogul Oprah Winfrey, CEO Weekly Top 10 Influential People In 2021 alongside Billionaires Jeff Bezos and Beyonce' and many more. She is also apart of The Forbes Next 1000 Class of 2021 in partnership with Square. This first-of-its-kind initiative celebrates bold and inspiring entrepreneurs who are redefining what it means to run a business. Lastly, she is a proud member of The Chancellors Round Table at North Carolina A&T State University.

She is a proud member of Delta Sigma Theta Sorority Incorporated, and a member of Alpha Phi Omega. She is very involved in her community, organizations and non-profits. Currently, she is the Co-Founder of Sweetheart Scholars Non-profit Organization 501 (C-3) along with three other powerful women. This scholarship is given out annually to African American Females from her hometown of Wadesboro, North Carolina who are attending college to help with their expenses. Dr. Little believes it takes a village to raise a child and to never forget where you come from. Dr. Little is a strong believer in giving back to her community. She believes our young ladies need vision, direction, and strong mentorship. She is the CEO/Founder/Visionary Author of The HBCU Experience Movement, LLC the first Black-owned company to launch books written and published by prominent alumni throughout the world who attended Historically Black Colleges & Universities. As authors, they share a powerful collection of stories on how their unique college experience has molded them into the people they are today. Our company's goal is to change the narrative by sharing Black stories and investing financially back into our HBCUs to increase young alumni giving and enrollment. The Award-Winning Best Selling Authors won the Black Authors Matter TV Award May 2021 and winner of the International Book Awards by The American Book Fest. The books are also apart of the WorldCat.Org the world's largest network of library content and services. Dr. Little is also the Editor and Chief of Creating Your Seat At The Table International Magazine, Advisor for She Wins Society, and Writing and Publishing Coach for the WILDE Winner's Circle.

She is the Founder and Owner of T.A.L.K Radio & TV Network, LLC. Airs in over 167 countries, streamed LIVE on Facebook, YouTube, Twitter and Periscope. Broadcasting and Media Production Company. This live entertainment platform is for new or existing radio shows, television shows, or other electronic media outlets, to air content from a centralized source. All news, information or music shared on this platform are solely the responsibility of the station/radio owner. She is also the Owner and Creator of Creative Broadcasting Radio Station the station of "unlimited possibilities" and Podcast, Radio/TV Host. She is also one of the hosts of the new TV Show Daytime Drama National Syndicated Television Show which will be aired on Comcast Channel 19 and ATT Channel 99 in 19 Middle

Tennessee Counties. It will also air on The United Broadcasting Network, The Damascus Roads Broadcasting Network, and Roku. She is CEO/Founder/Visionary Author of The HBCU Experience Movement LLC and CEO/Founder of Little Publishing LLC.

Dr. Little is a 15X Award-Winning Best Selling Author of "Dear Fear, Volume 2 18 Powerful Lessons Of Living Your Best Life Outside Of Fear", "The Gyrlfriend Code Volume 1", "I Survived", "Girl Get Up, and Win", "Glambitious Guide to Being An Entrepreneur", The Price of Greatness, The Making Of A Successful Business Woman, and "Hello Queen". She is a Co-Host for The Tamie Collins Markee Radio Show, Award-Winning Entrepreneur, Reflection Contributor for the book "NC Girls Living In A Maryland World, Sales/Marketing/Contributing Writer/Event Correspondent for SwagHer Magazine, Contributing Writer for MizCEO Magazine, Contributing Editor for SheIs Magazine, ContributingWriter/ National Sales Executive for Courageous Woman Magazine, Contributing Writer for Upwords International Magazine (India), Contributing Writer/Global Partner for Powerhouse Global International Magazine(London), Host of "Creating Your Seat At The Table", Host of "Authors On The Rise", Co-Host Glambitious Podcast, Partner/Visionary Author of The Gyrlfriend Code The Sorority Edition along with The Gyrlfriend Collective, LLC and CEO/Visionary Author of The HBCU Experience The North Carolina A&T State University Edition. She has been on many different Podcasts, TV Shows, Magazines, and Radio Shows. Lastly, she has received awards such as "Author Of The Month", The Executive Citation of Anne Arundel County, Maryland Award which was awarded by the County Executive Steuart L. Pittman, Top 28 Influential Business Pioneers for K.I.S.H Magazine Spring 2019 Edition. She has been featured in SwagHer Magazine, Power20Magazine Glambitious, Sheen Magazine, All About Inspire Magazine, Formidable Magazine, BRAG Magazine, Sheen Magazine, Front Cover of MizCEO Magazine November 2019, Front Cover for UpWords Magazine October 2019 Edition,

Courageous Woman Magazine, Courageous Woman Special Speakers Edition November 2019, Influence Magazine, Featured/Interviewed On a National Syndicated Television Show HBCU 101 on Aspire TV, Dynasty of Dreamers K.I.S.H Magazine Spring 2019 Edition, Dynasty of Dreamers K.I.S.H Magazine September 2019 Edition, Front Cover of Courageous Magazine December 2019, Front Cover of Doz International Magazine January 2020, Top 28 Influential Business Pioneers for K.I.S.H Magazine, Power20 Magazine Glambitious January 2020, Power20 Magazine Glambitious February 2020, Featured in Powerhouse Global International London Magazine March 2020 edition, Featured in National Boss Magazine October 2020 Edition, Featured in Sheen Magazine February 2020 as one of "The Top 20 Women To Be On The Lookout For In 2020, BlackNews.com, BlackBusiness.com, Front Cover She Speaks Magazine August 2020, Front Cover National Boss Magazine November 2020, BlackNewsScoop.com, Awarded National Women's Empowerment Ministry "Young, Gifted, & Black Award" February 2020 which honors and celebrate women in business such as Senior Level Executives, Entrepreneurs and CEO's below age 40 for their creativity and business development. Featured in National Women Empowerment Magazine 2020, Featured in Black Enterprise 2020, Featured on Fox, NBC, CBS 2020, Featured/Interviewed on National Syndicated Television The Black Report on Fox Soul TV, Front Cover for National Boss Magazine 2020, Speaker at The Black College Expo 2020, Speaker for Creative CEO's summit January 2021, International Speaker for Living Your Dream Life Summit 2021, Speaker for Elite Business Women Powershift Conference 2021, Keynote Speaker/Host/Panelist for The Bella, The Brand & Her Bag Wealth Summit 2021, Speaker for The Unstoppable You Summit January 2021, Speaker for Marketing Mastery Summit for Glambitious 2021, Speaker for Crown Yourself Conference January 2021, Featured in Sheen Print Magazine 2021, Speaker at Door Dash Virtual Black History Month Celebration, Speaker for Day Of Aggie Generations with North Carolina A&T State University, 2021 Woman of Black Excellence

Honoree, Guest/Speaker on podcast The Happy Hour Show, Speaker for the Phoenix Jack & Jill HBCU Author Showcase, Guest/Speaker on The JMosley Show, Contributing Author for "Prayers For The Entrepreneurial Woman Book", Speaker for Creative Con, Recognized as one of Today's Black History Makers, Speaker at From Paper to Profits conference, Press Conference/Press for "Don't Waste Your Petty" Movie, Press Conference/Press for Mahalia Jackson movie, Speaker for HerStory Women's Global Empowerment Summit, Speaker for HerStory Women Who Lead Conference, Speaker for Stepping N2 Sisterhood Sharing Winning Secrets Virtual Summit, Speaker for I AM Glambitious Virtual Conference, Speaker for Black Authors Matter TV show, Speaker for Thought Leaders Global Virtual Summit, Speaker for A Conversation with Floyd Marshall Jr., Black Authors Matter TV Award Winner, Speaker for Sheen Talk, Foreword Author for the anthology "It Cost To Be The Boss", Top 50 Most Influential Women recognized by VIP Global Magazine, Speaker at Black Writers Weekend, Speaker on The GameChangers With Angela Ward Show Keynote Speaker for Blacks In Nonprofits Conference, Speaker for Leap Conference, Speaker on Pass The Mic Sis, Speaker for From Purpose to Profit Summit, Speaker on The Been Worthy Podcast, Speaker/Host for The Miz CEO Graduation and TEDx Host as well to name a few.

Dr. Little received her undergraduate degree in English from North Carolina A&T State University. Next, she received her Master's Degree in Industrial Organizational Psychology. She has received her Doctorate in Humanitarian and Leadership as well. Dr. Little is a mover and shaker and she continuously pushes herself to be better than she was yesterday. She gives GOD all the credit for everything that has happened in her life. She has strong faith and determination to be great. She believes her only competition is herself. Her favorite scripture is Philippians 4:13 "I can do all things through Christ who strengthens me".

ROYALL M. MACK, SR.

One Aggies Truth
Royall M. Mack, Sr.

The Beginning

On Feb. 1, 1960, four Black college students sat down at a white-only lunch counter in Greensboro, N.C. I was 14 years young at that time, entering my sophomore year in high school. I paid no attention to civil unrest. But my father, Ernest E. Mack Sr. and mother, Thelma S. Montague Mack, saw a nonviolent movement consisting of Black youth sit-ins advancing through the South. They clipped articles from Black newspapers, Ebony and Jet magazines.

Fast forward to the spring of 1964, my senior year of high school. Where I would attend college was being discussed. Several predominantly white institutions (PWIs) and three historically Black colleges and universities (HBCUs) had expressed interest through athletic scholarships. Their focus was primarily on my skills with a basketball and baseball. I was thrilled at the thought of a career in either of the two.

The Decision

On the evening of May 16, 1964, my father and mother sat me down and said they had made a decision as to where I would attend college. I had given input for weeks expressing my choices ranking them 1, 2 and 3. Thinking it would be one or my three choices – two predominantly white institutions or Hampton Institute where my brother was a rising junior. I was eager to hear their (really, our) decision.

When they said A&T College, as it was known in 1964, I was shocked, heartbroken and saddened. A&T was not even on my list. I had never heard of the college, but my father and mother were very well acquainted with it. Two well-respected families in town had sent their sons to A&T. When I asked my dad how he had made up his mind, he handed me three articles: one from the Baltimore Journal and Guide, one from Ebony and the third from the Richmond (Virginia) Times-Dispatch. These articles had a different spin on the Woolworth sit-ins and subsequent demonstrations to end segregation.

My dad added, "Your life is not to be one of a professional athlete. Those suggesting you could be were simply not telling you the TRUTH. I know you, and believe me, you are not that good. A&T College is creating men and women who are making a difference in this country – a better place for your mother and I and people of color. I hope we live long enough to see it." He then asked me to read the articles and stop pouting.

Thus, my journey at A&T College began in August 1964. Honesty is more than simply the absence of lies. It deals also in truthfulness, candor, forthrightness and righteousness. These values have always been among my family's most cherished values – values that continued to be reinforced at A&T College.

My Time at A&T

Over time, I saw the wisdom of my parents' decision. The athletes who came to A&T in 1964 had to be some of the best in the country – tall, big, fast and smart. Being from a small town in Virginia (West Point), I had not seen men possessing such athletic qualities. My father was correct: I could not compete. I did manage a successful baseball opportunity at the college. My head coach, Mel Groomes, proved to be more than a coach. He became a mentor in teaching self-worth, making a difference in the world full of injustice, and my important role as an African American man. Like my father, he told me the TRUTH.

Other TRUTH tellers during my years at A&T were:

- Mr. James Barber

- Dr. William Bell

- Mr. Ellis Corbitt

- Lt. Col. William G. Goode

- Mrs. Ruth Gore

- Dr. Lewis (Professor and Instructor, Western Civilization)

- The Rev. Cleo McCoy

- Mr. Richard Moore

- Miss Marguarite Porter

- Dr. Albert W. Spruill

- Dr. Morris Stroud

These men and women were truth tellers during my years at A&T. They destroyed myths about inferiority and lies that abounded about African Americans and armed me with historical facts about Black accomplishments, as well as the truth about my capabilities and my capacity to contribute. They continued – like my father – to tell me the TRUTH.

HBCUs' Values
They Teach Tenacity

Tenacious people are nearly impossible to defeat, turn down or turn around; they're as unyielding as a summer day is long – which is a good thing. Much of the human progress and the future of African-Americans is dependent upon tenacity, an essential ingredient in any formula for success. HBCUs teach tenacity in a way that is not aggressive or in-your-face. Without tenacity, much that we now take for granted would have never been achieved. It would be left undiscovered or unknown. There are two types of tenacious people: big players on the world stage, who struggle to survive and lead lives of quiet dignity, and movers and shakers – key players who bring about momentous change whether in corporate America, on battlefields, in laboratories or in local school board meetings. HBCUs have produced its share of each. HBCUs, take a bow!

They Teach Faith and Love

Faith has moved mountains, built empires, defeated invincible armies, stirred billions of people through the ages and generated indescribable love. Aside from these, what more powerful virtues could there be in this world? Ultimately, faith and love allow us to soar spiritually. Yet, since we also live in this world, faith and love should plant our feet on solid ground. They should anchor us socially and override a framework for moral reasoning. HBCUs have done that and more since their inception and continue to do so today.

HBCUs are as vital today as they have ever been – not just for African-Americans, but for all people. In a society, rife with turmoil, consumerism and misery, faith and love still bring joy, peace, fulfillment and kindness to millions and they are exhibited at every level of African American culture and life.

"The Circle of Faith" by Tiaudra Riley

I

have faith in you

because I trust you. I trust you

because I like you. I understand you

because I care for you. I care for you

because I am a part of you. I am part of you

because I depend on you. I depend on you

because I am honest with you. I am honest

with you because I can talk to you. I can talk

to you because I am for you. I am for you

because I need you. I need you because I

love you. I love you because I believe

in you. I believe in you because I

have faith in

you.

This poem was not written for HBCUs, but the words fit perfectly.

A&T State University, Our Friend

How strong are your allegiances? Are you someone's protégé, closest friend or trusted companion? If so, you know the world admires and respects an abiding faithfulness to people, duty and institutions. Our most sacred relationships and our finest organizations are built on a bedrock of allegiances. Like signposts along life's roads we travel, our loyalties announce our friendships, commitments, what we really care about and will remain devoted to.

AT&T State University has been a friend to thousands of students. Thousands of lives have been positively impacted by students who have graced her halls. It is now time for all of us to show our love to this beautiful lady by showing our allegiance to her with our money.

Giving Back to Impact Others

Do you have compassion for others? Do you want to ensure A&T State University is strong and continues to produce leaders? If so, you need a dash of tenderness, a little sympathy and a connection – a sort of moral umbilical cord for the next generation of humanity and students who desire to attend A&T State University.

Compassion for our university might well be the most humane moral value of all. It has none of the contemptuous sorrow characterized by pity; it is shaped by great concern, sometimes as much for others as for ourselves. We feel compassion when we feel a need to help others who need a helping hand to a better life. The river of compassion, shaped by powerful currents of misery and hope, runs deep and strong through Black America. Our HBCUs serve as lighthouses to guide us to better lives. We alumni need to show concern, compassion and gratitude to our alma mater. We must do what we can, as often as we can, to ensure the university remains strong now and in the future.

About Royall M. Mack, Sr.

ROYALL M. MACK SR. is a retired corporate officer of The Gillette Company, based in Boston, and is a veteran of sales, finance, marketing and product development functions worldwide. Royall was selected by Gillette's Board of Directors to lead the consolidation of all Gillette North American merchandising functions, including blade/razor, Duracell, personal care, Oral-B and Braun divisions. Royall developed branding for Gillette Giving worldwide. Prior to his retirement after 38 years of service, he was named corporate officer and senior vice president of Civic Affairs where he led Gillette's philanthropic programs worldwide.

While at Gillette, Royall became vice president of Ethnic Markets, a $1 billion ethnic consumer market. He assumed additional responsibility for Gillette's $500 million government market worldwide group.

Royall revamped Gillette's Minority Purchasing Program, increasing purchases from minority vendors from $11.6 million to $53.6 million. Consequently, Royall earned The Gillette Company "Minority Supplier of the Year" recognition in New England. The program soared to $68 million, earning Gillette a second Minority Supplier Award.

Royall has served on numerous boards and community organizations such as Bridge Over Troubled Waters Inc., Boston; Executive Leadership Council and Foundation, Alexandria, Virginia; National Black College Hall of Fame Foundation, Atlanta; Association of Technology Management and Applied Engineering (ATMAE), Ann Arbor, Michigan; Chair of the Board of Visitors and Chair of the College of Arts and Sciences Advisory Board, both at

North Carolina Agricultural and Technical State University, Greensboro, North Carolina.

Royall was selected by then-Governor of Massachusetts Deval Patrick to serve as a trustee at Middlesex Community College, the largest community college in the state. He later was named chairman of the board. While serving in that role, Royall focused on helping to add a strategic focus in K-12 standards for the community college system, to bolster student success initiatives, and to strengthen workforce development ties with other academic institutions and the corporate community.

Royall's awards include the prestigious Thurgood Marshall Leadership Award, induction into the National Black College Hall of Fame, Phi Kappa Phi Honor Society, Beta Gamma Sigma Business Honor Society, Presidential Award as a Distinguished Alumnus of North Carolina A&T State University, Business Executive of the Year, New England's Business Council, and Honorary Doctor of Humanities from North Carolina A&T State University. Royall served as co-chair of North Carolina A&T State University Capital Campaign Committee (2016-2020); past chair of the Pleasant Grove Foundation, Cary, North Carolina (2019-2021); Gentleman's Mutual Investment Club (GMIC), Cary, (2019-present); and Dream Academy Leadership Team, Cary, (2018-present).

Royall earned his Bachelor of Science in history from North Carolina A&T State University and successfully matriculated through the Advanced Management Program (AMP 109) at Harvard University.

Royall has this message for all, which he learned from his grandparents, parents, N.C. A&T and life experiences:

The preservation of a people, their culture and their institutions are dependent on the persistence of its citizens to:

- Know, preserve, and teach the history

- Have a vision for the future growth of its people, culture, and institutions

- Sacrifice for what is envisioned, but not yet seen

- Invest time, treasure and energy in the young (in age and at heart)

- Understand money, the use of credit and then learn how to make them work for your benefit*(10, 10, 10, and 70)

- Display respect, grace, truth and integrity at all times

- Trust in God to do His Will, His Way and in His Time

  *(10% church, 10% charitable organizations/institutions, 10% investments, 70% living expenses)

Royall's basic reading list:

- "The African American Book of Values" edited and with commentary by Steven Barboza

- "Man Alive: Transforming Your Seven Primal Needs into a Powerful Spiritual Life" by Patrick Morley

- "Dark Money: The Hidden History of the Billionaires Behind the Rise of the Radical Right" by Jane Mayer

- "The Sword and The Shield: The Revolutionary Lives of Malcolm X and Martin Luther King Jr." by Peniel E. Joseph

- "Experiencing God Together: How Your Connection with Others Deepens Your Relationship with God" by Tony Evans

- "White Fragility" by Robin DiAngelo

In June 2016, Royall and his bride of 42 years, Valerie, relocated to Durham, North Carolina, from Andover, Massachusetts, to be closer to their five children, nine grandchildren and two great-grandchildren. Royall and Valerie are disciples at Pleasant Grove Church in Cary.

My appreciation for hard work began with my grandparents and parents. Work ethic and self-esteem were driven into me and have proven to be the most valuable gifts given to me at home and at A&T. When we work hard and smart, we show others – especially our children – that work is worth their time and effort. Dr. Lewis, whose tests were given in little blue books, taught me that when we really enjoy what we're doing, we prove that we can be very good at it and it has intrinsic value. The lessons I learned about honesty and working hard and smart can be applied to almost any occupation – whether you're in high school or a university student, a secretary or surgeon. The same principle applies: Enjoy what you do. One of my greatest irritants is having to tell people my degree is from N.C. A&T – not AT&T!

Table of Contents

continued...

DR. JUDY NAZIRAH RASHID

Foreword
Dr. Judy Nazirah Rashid

Much has been written about the historical origins of Historically Black Colleges and Universities, commonly referred to as HBCUs. There have been many ambitious attempts to examine the historical inception of HBCUs in the United States, their present role in higher education, and their potential future. Research chronicles the pursuit of higher education by free Black people in the North to a wide array of efforts to educate freed slaves in the South after the Civil War including the establishment of land grant colleges. These efforts included those of the Freedman's Bureau established in 1865 and of private groups such as northern White missionary societies and Black churches. These glorious institutions have remained a vital part of the American higher education landscape for more than 150 years. However, we must remember that....

"Until lions have their own historians, the stories of the hunt will always glorify the hunter." –African Proverb

As a result, this anthology is a first hand, ambitious attempt for alumni to detail their OWNstory and not rely on HIStory; the accounts in this book are about us by us.

This book is an attempt to highlight, through the alumni own perspectives, the broader, deeper, and more unifying topics of engagement, perseverance, and achievement. These experiences serve as beacons of pride for HBCUs fostered through rich undergraduate experiences such as service learning/community service opportunities, academic accomplishments, student activities, student leadership development, and civic engagement. Consequently, these accounts translate to stellar alumni accomplishments which serve to defend the honor of this historical group of institutions for posterity.

North Carolina Agricultural and Technical State University is a proud member of this world-renowned family of black colleges and universities. We are known for that good 'ole Aggie Spirit birthed in 1891. We are the sons and daughters of those yearning to be free. We are the ones who grew up and dared to **A**ssemble and **T**ake over and fight for the least of these, and give back, and pull up. Each one reaches one, teach one to become and fulfill their God given potential. We **A**chieve **G**reat **G**oals **I**n **E**verything (AGGIE). We **P**roduce **R**enowned **I**ndividuals **D**edicated to **E**xcellence (PRIDE). Four of our students, as Freshmen in 1960, sat down so that the world could stand up. We were born and bred to uphold the motto of our first graduation class as we proclaimed NO STEPS BACKWARDS.

Still today, we march, we sit, we walk, we write, we speak out, we question, we contest, we challenge, we probe, and we demand as we march on till victory is won. We are destined to effect change. We know that…

"When your roots are so deep, there is no reason to fear the wind."
–African Proverb

Dr. Judy Rashid
NC A&T '74 and '91

About Dr. Judy Nazirah Rashid

Dr. Judy Nazirah Rashid is Founder and CEO of <u>Skills Training and Development Consulting Services</u> (STADCS). She has been involved in education for the last 44 years as teacher and school principal (K-12), senior student affairs administrator, and as adjunct faculty in Liberal Studies (Conflict Resolution) and the PhD Program in Leadership Studies. As the Associate Vice Chancellor for Student Affairs, she supervised Student Conduct, International Students, Veterans and Student Disability Support Services, Multicultural Students, Greek Life, and Student Government where she also supervised the University Queens for 20 years.

She recently retired as the Associate Vice Chancellor for Student Affairs / Dean of Students from her undergraduate alma mater, North Carolina A&T State University. Currently she serves as an Adjunct Assistant Professor in the Dept. of Adult Education and Leadership Studies.

Since 1989, Dr. Rashid has been professionally involved in conflict management education and training including international conflict resolution in South Africa. For almost two decades, she has garnered financial educational support for South African youth and adults. In December 2019, a recently erected building in Vanderjilpark, South Africa was named the Dr. Judy Rashid Education and Leadership Center.

Dr. Rashid received her Bachelor of Science and Masters' degrees (both summa cum laude) from North Carolina A&T and her doctoral degree in higher education administration from North Carolina State University in Raleigh. She holds certification in both interaction management and performance management from the State of North Carolina, advanced training in teaching negotiation in the organization from Harvard University, complete course training in N.C. Law for Non-Attorney Mediators, Mediation Certification Training/N.C. Superior Court Mediated Settlement Conferences, and Mediation Certification Training/Equal Employment Opportunity Commission.

Dr. Rashid is a member of the N.C. Bar Association (Dispute Resolution Section) and the NC Association of Retired Governmental Employees. Dr. Rashid dedicates her civic life through service to the less fortunate and is a Charter Member of both the National Museum of African American History and Culture of Washington D.C. and of the International African American Museum in Charleston, S.C.

Dr. Rashid is married and has two adult sons and an outstanding grandson.

DR. ASHLEY LITTLE

Introduction
Dr. Ashley Little

Historically Black Colleges and Universities are a source of accomplishment and great pride for the African-American Community as well as the entire nation. HBCU'S serve as empowerment, belonging and a sense of self-determination that black americans have struggled to attain as a whole. I am so thankful I attended North Carolina Agricultural & Technical State University. North Carolina A&T made me the person I am today. The family Environment, Black Excellence, Surrounded by people of many different cultures and races, The Greatest Homecoming On Earth known as (GHOE), and most of all knowing I can go anywhere in the world and an Aggie will have my back.

North Carolina Agricultural & Technical State University has prepared and instilled in me I can create the life I want to live. I am able to create my seat at tables with people who do not look like me and most of all build my own tables. My journey at A&T has been a blessing from the staff and faculty, the lessons and the wins, family environment, mentors, and most of all the life long friendships that have turned into family.

My goal is to create a global movement of Aggies to continue to share their stories each year to give back to the Prestigious North Carolina A&T State University. The authors hopes are to encourage, uplift, support, and pave the way for the next generation by sharing their stories and experiences of how North Carolina A&T State University has molded them into the people they are today. We have to continue to invest in our HBCU'S and continue to create our seats at the table. "It is important for HBCU Grads to give back, share and document our stories. Our voices and stories are powerful and need to be heard".

The HBCU Experience North Carolina A&T State University Edition is documented stories from Aggie Trailblazers throughout the nation. This book will highlight Aggies from many different eras. We hope every reader is touched by the stories and feel the Aggie Pride. Lastly, we hope to change and save lives by encouraging every reader to see it through. Aggie Born, Aggie Bred, and When We Die We Will Be Aggie Dead!! Aggie Dead!! Aggie Pride!!!

Visionary Author
Dr. Ashley Little

About Dr. Ashley Little

Dr. Ashley Little is The CEO/Founder of Ashley Little Enterprises, LLC which encompasses her Media, Consulting Work, Writing, Ghost Writing, Book Publishing, Book Coaching, Project Management, Magazine, Public Relations & Marketing, and Empowerment Speaking. In addition, she is an Award-Winning Serial Entrepreneur, TV/Radio Host, TEDx Speaker, International Speaker, Keynote Speaker, Media Maven, Journalist, Writer, Host, Philanthropist, Business Coach, Investor, Advisor for She Wins Society and 15X Award-Winning Best Selling Author. As seen on Black Enterprise(2X), Sheen Magazine (Print and Online), Sheen Talk, Voyage ATL, Fox Soul TV, NBC, Fox, CBS, BlackNews.Com, Shoutout Miami, Shoutout Atlanta, TEDx Speaker, Morning Star, Yahoo Finance, Heart and Soul, The Book of Sean, HBCU Times, VIP Global Magazine, The Black Report, Vocal, Ted.com, Medium, Soul Wealth, Hustle and Soul, BlackBusiness.com, New York Weekly Top 10 Hardest Working CEOs alongside Billionaire Mark Cuban, US Insiders Top 10 Women Entrepreneurs alongside Billionaire and Media Mogul Oprah Winfrey, CEO Weekly Top 10 Influential People In 2021 alongside Billionaires Jeff Bezos and Beyonce' and many more. She is also apart of The Forbes Next 1000 Class of 2021 in partnership with Square. This first-of-its-kind initiative celebrates bold and inspiring entrepreneurs who are redefining what it means to run a business. Lastly, she is a proud member of The Chancellors Round Table at North Carolina A&T State University.

She is a proud member of Delta Sigma Theta Sorority Incorporated, and a member of Alpha Phi Omega. She is very involved in her community, organizations and non-profits. Currently, she is the Co-Founder of Sweetheart Scholars Non-profit Organization 501 (C-3) along with three other powerful women. This scholarship is given out annually to African American Females from her hometown of Wadesboro, North Carolina who are attending college to help with their expenses. Dr. Little believes it takes a village to raise a child and to never forget where you come from. Dr. Little is a strong believer in giving back to her community. She believes our young ladies need vision, direction, and strong mentorship. She is the CEO/Founder/Visionary Author of The HBCU Experience Movement, LLC the first Black-owned company to launch books written and published by prominent alumni throughout the world who attended Historically Black Colleges & Universities. As authors, they share a powerful collection of stories on how their unique college experience has molded them into the people they are today. Our company's goal is to change the narrative by sharing Black stories and investing financially back into our HBCUs to increase young alumni giving and enrollment. The Award-Winning Best Selling Authors won the Black Authors Matter TV Award May 2021 and winner of the International Book Awards by The American Book Fest. The books are also apart of the WorldCat.Org the world's largest network of library content and services. Dr. Little is also the Editor and Chief of Creating Your Seat At The Table International Magazine, Advisor for She Wins Society, and Writing and Publishing Coach for the WILDE Winner's Circle.

She is the Founder and Owner of T.A.L.K Radio & TV Network, LLC. Airs in over 167 countries, streamed LIVE on Facebook, YouTube, Twitter and Periscope. Broadcasting and Media Production Company. This live entertainment platform is for new or existing radio shows, television shows, or other electronic media outlets, to air content from a centralized source. All news, information or music shared on this platform are solely the responsibility of the station/radio owner. She is also the Owner and Creator of Creative Broadcasting Radio Station the station of "unlimited possibilities" and Podcast, Radio/TV Host. She is also one of the hosts of the new TV Show Daytime Drama National Syndicated Television Show which will be aired on Comcast Channel 19 and ATT Channel 99 in 19 Middle

Tennessee Counties. It will also air on The United Broadcasting Network, The Damascus Roads Broadcasting Network, and Roku. She is CEO/Founder/Visionary Author of The HBCU Experience Movement LLC and CEO/Founder of Little Publishing LLC.

Dr. Little is a 15X Award-Winning Best Selling Author of "Dear Fear, Volume 2 18 Powerful Lessons Of Living Your Best Life Outside Of Fear", "The Gyrlfriend Code Volume 1", "I Survived", "Girl Get Up, and Win", "Glambitious Guide to Being An Entrepreneur", The Price of Greatness, The Making Of A Successful Business Woman, and "Hello Queen". She is a Co-Host for The Tamie Collins Markee Radio Show, Award-Winning Entrepreneur, Reflection Contributor for the book "NC Girls Living In A Maryland World, Sales/Marketing/Contributing Writer/Event Correspondent for SwagHer Magazine, Contributing Writer for MizCEO Magazine, Contributing Editor for SheIs Magazine, ContributingWriter/ National Sales Executive for Courageous Woman Magazine, Contributing Writer for Upwords International Magazine (India), Contributing Writer/Global Partner for Powerhouse Global International Magazine(London), Host of "Creating Your Seat At The Table", Host of "Authors On The Rise", Co-Host Glambitious Podcast, Partner/Visionary Author of The Gyrlfriend Code The Sorority Edition along with The Gyrlfriend Collective, LLC and CEO/Visionary Author of The HBCU Experience The North Carolina A&T State University Edition. She has been on many different Podcasts, TV Shows, Magazines, and Radio Shows. Lastly, she has received awards such as "Author Of The Month", The Executive Citation of Anne Arundel County, Maryland Award which was awarded by the County Executive Steuart L. Pittman, Top 28 Influential Business Pioneers for K.I.S.H Magazine Spring 2019 Edition. She has been featured in SwagHer Magazine, Power20Magazine Glambitious, Sheen Magazine, All About Inspire Magazine, Formidable Magazine, BRAG Magazine, Sheen Magazine, Front Cover of MizCEO Magazine November 2019, Front Cover for UpWords Magazine October 2019 Edition,

Courageous Woman Magazine, Courageous Woman Special Speakers Edition November 2019, Influence Magazine, Featured/Interviewed On a National Syndicated Television Show HBCU 101 on Aspire TV, Dynasty of Dreamers K.I.S.H Magazine Spring 2019 Edition, Dynasty of Dreamers K.I.S.H Magazine September 2019 Edition, Front Cover of Courageous Magazine December 2019, Front Cover of Doz International Magazine January 2020, Top 28 Influential Business Pioneers for K.I.S.H Magazine, Power20 Magazine Glambitious January 2020, Power20 Magazine Glambitious February 2020, Featured in Powerhouse Global International London Magazine March 2020 edition, Featured in National Boss Magazine October 2020 Edition, Featured in Sheen Magazine February 2020 as one of "The Top 20 Women To Be On The Lookout For In 2020, BlackNews.com, BlackBusiness.com, Front Cover She Speaks Magazine August 2020, Front Cover National Boss Magazine November 2020, BlackNewsScoop.com, Awarded National Women's Empowerment Ministry "Young, Gifted, & Black Award" February 2020 which honors and celebrate women in business such as Senior Level Executives, Entrepreneurs and CEO's below age 40 for their creativity and business development. Featured in National Women Empowerment Magazine 2020, Featured in Black Enterprise 2020, Featured on Fox, NBC, CBS 2020, Featured/Interviewed on National Syndicated Television The Black Report on Fox Soul TV, Front Cover for National Boss Magazine 2020, Speaker at The Black College Expo 2020, Speaker for Creative CEO's summit January 2021, International Speaker for Living Your Dream Life Summit 2021, Speaker for Elite Business Women Powershift Conference 2021, Keynote Speaker/Host/Panelist for The Bella, The Brand & Her Bag Wealth Summit 2021, Speaker for The Unstoppable You Summit January 2021, Speaker for Marketing Mastery Summit for Glambitious 2021, Speaker for Crown Yourself Conference January 2021, Featured in Sheen Print Magazine 2021, Speaker at Door Dash Virtual Black History Month Celebration, Speaker for Day Of Aggie Generations with North Carolina A&T State University, 2021 Woman of Black Excellence

Honoree, Guest/Speaker on podcast The Happy Hour Show, Speaker for the Phoenix Jack & Jill HBCU Author Showcase, Guest/Speaker on The JMosley Show, Contributing Author for "Prayers For The Entrepreneurial Woman Book", Speaker for Creative Con, Recognized as one of Today's Black History Makers, Speaker at From Paper to Profits conference, Press Conference/Press for "Don't Waste Your Petty" Movie, Press Conference/Press for Mahalia Jackson movie, Speaker for HerStory Women's Global Empowerment Summit, Speaker for HerStory Women Who Lead Conference, Speaker for Stepping N2 Sisterhood Sharing Winning Secrets Virtual Summit, Speaker for I AM Glambitious Virtual Conference, Speaker for Black Authors Matter TV show, Speaker for Thought Leaders Global Virtual Summit, Speaker for A Conversation with Floyd Marshall Jr., Black Authors Matter TV Award Winner, Speaker for Sheen Talk, Foreword Author for the anthology "It Cost To Be The Boss", Top 50 Most Influential Women recognized by VIP Global Magazine, Speaker at Black Writers Weekend, Speaker on The GameChangers With Angela Ward Show Keynote Speaker for Blacks In Nonprofits Conference, Speaker for Leap Conference, Speaker on Pass The Mic Sis, Speaker for From Purpose to Profit Summit, Speaker on The Been Worthy Podcast, Speaker/Host for The Miz CEO Graduation and TEDx Host as well to name a few.

Dr. Little received her undergraduate degree in English from North Carolina A&T State University. Next, she received her Master's Degree in Industrial Organizational Psychology. She has received her Doctorate in Humanitarian and Leadership as well. Dr. Little is a mover and shaker and she continuously pushes herself to be better than she was yesterday. She gives GOD all the credit for everything that has happened in her life. She has strong faith and determination to be great. She believes her only competition is herself. Her favorite scripture is Philippians 4:13 "I can do all things through Christ who strengthens me".

DESMOND J. STOWE

HBCU Raised, Aggie Made
Desmond J. Stowe

If it had not been for Historically Black Colleges and Universities (HBCU), the person I am today would not exist. As a military child, I grew up traveling the world and seeing different cultures across the globe. Although this experience as a young child helped build my character and a strong sense of diversity; it was not until I experienced my own culture, at its best, that I felt most alive.

Having a love for HBCUs came very easy for me. Most of my family members attended HBCUs, Barber Scotia College, Livingstone College and North Carolina A&T State University (NCA&T) to name a few. I was exposed to all of these schools through homecomings. Both my mother and father (Ernest and Melanie Stowe) are active alumni of Livingstone College. They both exposed me to campus tours and these opportunities are where I came to fall in love with the HBCU experience. It was the band, cheerleaders, and Greeks that really caught my attention. As a child I was a member of the Order of the Knights of Pythagoras. The Order of the Knights of Pythagoras is a community-based mentoring organization sponsored by Prince Hall Masons, Inc. It's dedicated to the Fatherhood of God and the Universal Brotherhood of Man. During the summers they took us to different HBCUs for a week of leadership training. By attending this program I not only visited but stayed in dorm rooms at Fayetteville State University, NC Central, Elizabeth City State University, and NC A&T. Thanks to my grandfather David Elmore Steele Sr., who made sure I went on the college trip with The Knights, by my high school, I had made up my mind that a HBCU was for me. Not only did he make sure I went, he took fifteen other young men, every summer, to a different HBCU.

When the time came to apply for college, NC A&T was one of my top choices. I remember seeing the sign in the guidance counselor's office that said NC A&T. I went to see the admission person, Kim Mainly, and she told me A&T was hosting "Aggie Night" in Charlotte, NC. At this event on-site admissions and acceptances were granted. They gave us the full Aggie welcome in the Adams Mark Hotel. That night my mother took me there and I was one of two students that were accepted on the spot. The joy that I felt from that day forward has remained the same.

Once on campus, I jumped in full speed ahead. Although I went to a predominantly black high school, I had never seen so many people who looked and acted like me. I WAS IN LOVE. That fall I moved into Scott Hall B as a Public Relations major. Eager to get involved I joined the Verge Modeling Troupe and the cheerleading team. I really wanted to be the Aggie Dog Mascot, but they already had one at that time, and since the cheerleading team needed more males I tried out for the squad. Later on I did become the Aggie Mascot, and enjoyed every minute of it. In my heart there will always be joy in running the Aggie Flag around the stadium to show the love I have for my school. My Junior year I wanted to be more involved, so I ran for Mr. Aggie (Mr. A&T) and won. I could not believe that I won but I took full advantage of the moment by speaking to the community and building my platform as an Aggie Leader.

As a leader I was no stranger to most, as I already liked to talk to people and never met a stranger. It was in this role that I began to formalize the term "networking". My talking turned into branding, marketing and becoming the person I wanted to become. At NC A&T I was taught not what to think, but how to think. This led to me running for SGA president. Although I did not win the presidency, I remained active in student leadership. I used that experience to further my public relation career by landing an internship at Charlotte Mecklenburg School System public relations office. There I was able to work in the field and gain mentors to help me through challenging times.

Once my undergraduate life was done, guess what? I wanted more… more Aggie spirit. Not wanting to stay in my undergraduate field of study, Dr. Roselle Wilson and Denise Iverson-Payne took me in as a mentee and I enrolled back at NC A&T for my Master degree in Higher Education. Being no stranger to Aggie land I joined Kappa Alpha Psi® Fraternity, Incorporated - Greensboro Alumni Chapter, where I was able to continue the Greek life legacy in my family. I also became a graduate hall director in the Aggie Suite E, which began my career in over 15 years of Student Affairs. I admit I was so in love with A&T, I decided to work there full time. The Dean of Students (Dr. Judy Rashid) hired me as the Program assistant for Student Conduct. There I gained professional training under Ms. Donna Blue working with University policy and regulations. No this was not the most exciting job but it laid a solid foundation for my student affairs career. Because of the strong Aggie foundation, I have been able to spread my love for HBCUs by working at Lincoln University PA and Savannah State University.

My love for HBCUs is the reason why I serve on the board of National Association of Student Affairs Professionals (NASAP). This organization is on the leading edge regarding issues, solutions, and professional development opportunities for student affairs professionals serving at Historically Black Colleges and Universities and for those professionals who serve minority populations in diverse settings around the country. On this board I have committed to train student leaders at over 50 HBCUs through the association's Student Leadership Institute held annually. I truly believe if an HBCU was good enough for me, it is good enough for our future. The future of youth I do not know and the youth in my family are all bright when attending an HBCU. My aunt and uncle, Franklin Steele Sr. and Elaine Steele, and I adore NC A&T and our HBCU experience. Thus influencing my cousin, Franklin Steele III, to attend NC A&T. Our Aggie legacy continues this year as he begins his Freshman year.

Attending North Carolina, A&T has been one of my greatest accomplishments and has made me into the person I am today. As my Chancellor, the 9th Chancellor of NC A&T, Dr. James C. Renick said to me, "Aggies are second to none". Forever I will always be Aggie Born and Breed. Aggie Pride!!!!!!!!

About Desmond J. Stowe

Desmond J. Stowe is a native of Charlotte NC and come from a family legacy of HBCU graduates. Stowe is recognized as a student-centered, customer service-oriented and transformational leader. Mr. Stowe holds a bachelor and master's degrees from North Carolina Agricultural and Technical State University. He is a committed university administrator, motivational speaker and host/comedian. He is a Spring 2005 Initiate of the Greensboro Alumni Chapter Kappa Alpha Psi Fraternity Inc. and remains active in his local chapter as Polemarch (Savannah Alumni). Desmond lives by a quote "If a task once begun never rest until its done, be the labor large or small do it well or not at all".

RACHEL DANIELLE LATIMORE

A Monument Indeed
Rachel Danielle Latimore

Growing up, two shows were mandatory in my household, "The Cosby Show" and "A Different World." My mother, a single parent, always wanted to make sure that I was exposed to different opportunities for college. So, naturally, when it came time for me to choose schools I would be interested in attending, the schools that interested me the most were HBCU's. While I knew I couldn't attend Hillman because it was a fictional place, I wanted to ensure that I had an experience that would provide me the opportunity to feel like I was a part of a community that I belong to. To grow deeper in my own understanding of my culture and be at a school where excellence and academics were a priority. I chose North Carolina A&T State University because of Chancellor Renick. I heard about the innovative leadership he brought to the campus just a couple of years before it was time for me to attend, and I wanted to be a part of that legacy. It was such an exciting time for the University and one of the best decisions I've made in my life.

I remember my excitement on move-in day. I knew that I was joining a community that would feel like family. I drove up to the Barbee Hall, parked my car, and as my mother and I were about to move my items into my suite at 308 D, Barbee Hall, we were greeted by Chancellor Renick's wife. She was helping to move freshmen into their dorms and asked me if I needed help moving my TV into my suite. At that point, my mom felt even more confident in my choice to attend North Carolina A&T State University. Where else would you have the President's wife helping to move freshmen into their dorms?

My experience at A&T has had a lasting impression on both my career and personal life trajectories. On the campus of A&T, I learned about the power of community building, leadership, excellence, and a commitment to social change. I was an active student leader, a member of the Student Government Association, the Alpha Mu chapter of Delta Sigma Theta Sorority Incorporated. Also, I actively participated in service projects around Greensboro. Because of A&T's commitment to service, I learned so much about what it means to give your time, talent, and treasure to help improve the lives and experiences of others. In addition, I have vivid memories of learning about the history of our beloved University. Like many students, the history of our very own freedom fighters instilled within us a sense of pride and power. We felt like we could do anything if we worked together as a community. One of my most vivid memories of my sophomore year was when I was asked to give the prayer at our annual historic February 1 breakfast. It also happened to be the 50th year anniversary of the sit-in movement on February 1, 1960. I had the wonderful opportunity to meet the four freshmen who sat down at the counter in Woolworth's, sparking an entire sit-in movement across this country all the way to South Africa. The many opportunities that A&T afforded me to learn about our history, our culture, and the power that we held as students with our voices, I've carried with me throughout my career in different sectors, including social development, youth leadership development, public service, education, and social entrepreneurship.

In addition to the lessons I learned about community, I was also challenged academically with professors and courses that challenged my thinking and caused me to become a more thoughtful scholar. As a sociology and marketing major, I had the opportunity to learn about social scientists and best practices in business. Both of these disciplines set me up to build my career in public service, community-building, and social entrepreneurship. Through the confidence that I gained as a student at A&T, I continued my education and pursued a master's program at Case Western Reserve University, where I studied

Community and Social Development. During the same time, then, Senator Barack Obama was running for his first presidential term. In my most recent academic program, an Executive Master's in Public Administration at NYU Wagner, I've deepened the knowledge I gained at A&T about what it means to be a leader and public servant. I am currently finishing my doctoral research at New York University in the Department of Education, focusing on leadership and innovation at NYU Steinhardt. This has allowed me to explore new and innovative ways to lead organizations and teams in the social impact and innovation space. None of my career experiences and academic experiences would have been possible had it not been for the extraordinary examples that I saw in administrators, leaders, and peers with whom I was in community at A&T.

Out of all of my accomplishments, I am most proud of being the first person in my family to attend an HBCU. By doing so, I dispelled the myths about HBCUs and their value in our community and the power that they held academically. My experiences at A&T not only impacted me but my family and the generations that will come after me. I now have cousins who are excited about attending an HBCU, and some considering A&T as their top choice. I have no doubt that their experiences, while different, will be just as powerful. The lessons, relationships, and experiences that I had while attending A&T as a student and that I've experienced as an Alumni have left a lasting impression on me. I'm so grateful for my beloved North Carolina A&T State University, all of the people I met, and the wonderful experiences I've had. They have shaped me into the leader, public servant, entrepreneur, scholar, friend, and woman I am today.

About Rachel Danielle Latimore

A passionate and visionary leader, Rachel D. is deeply committed to driving innovation and impact towards the goal of sustainability throughout global communities. In both her professional and academic careers, she has centered her research and practice around leadership and social impact through a DEI, racial equity, and social justice lens.

Rachel D. has dedicated the breadth of her career to advancing social justice and economic empowerment for black, brown, and indigenous communities across the globe. She has over a decade of experience in the field of community development, social entrepreneurship, and finding talent in the pursuit of innovative solutions to global and domestic challenges and centers her work around advancing equitable support to proximate leaders in marginalized communities.

For six years, she served as a Goodwill Ambassador to the Republic of the Gambia where she worked with the Ministry of Women Affairs and Ministry of Youth & Sports to engage key stakeholders in building capacity in areas of leadership development, education, health, and social innovation.

She paired her field experience and expertise in communities of practice, community-building, leadership development, social entrepreneurship, philanthropy, and impact investing with advanced education, obtaining an Executive Masters in Public Administration at NYU's Robert F. Wagner School of Public Service.

Rachel D. manages Echoing Green's global Fellow community by building deeply collaborative and equitable community experiences for nearly 1,000 global social innovation leaders across various identities, sectors, and geographies.

She is currently a Social Sector Leadership Development Fellow and doctoral candidate at NYU's Steinhardt School of Culture, Education, and Human Development pursuing an EdD in Leadership and Innovation. Her research and dissertation focuses on creating equitable support models for global BIPOC leaders and entrepreneurs in the social innovation community.

JAMES WOODERT, III

Fulfilling
James Woodert, III

If I had to describe my experience at A&T in one word, it would be "fulfilling." I mean, I literally left no stone unturned. The guy who was involved in everything, that was me. The social introvert who loved to be where the people were, that was me. The first one in class and the first one at the party, that was me. I refused to ever miss a moment with the community of Aggies I surrounded myself with daily. These years were my wonder years, and for some reason, I always had it in my mind that these moments would not last forever. So, I made it my duty and responsibility to simply stay active. This is my story.

Summer of 2001, a kid out of Fayetteville, North Carolina, steps foot on the campus of A&T. Beside me stands my mother and siblings, just as excited for this new chapter in my life as I am. There were so many thoughts running through my mind at that very moment. Still, my priority was to get situated and send my family on their way. "Time to be an adult," I told myself or what I thought was an adult at 18 years old. Scott Hall B, the foundation of my college living experience, was quite an interesting stay. I met some of the dopest individuals at that dorm. One, in particular, was my next-door neighbor, Calvin Williams, Jr. Little did I know how important he was going to be to me later in life. Freshman year was a blast. I had never been surrounded by so many goal-oriented people that looked like me … that talked like me … that thought like me. I and A&T were a match made in heaven.

Second semester, freshman year, a lot of great things happened for me. I ran for Student Council of Scott Hall B, got involved in the Student Union Advisory Board (SUAB), and became a member of the best organization on campus, The Eta Chapter of Phi Beta Sigma, Fraternity, Inc. Talk about a home run year, whew! I thought I was the man after all of that. So, what else was left, right? Yeah, little did I know; there was so much more to college than just being involved in organizations. But I was definitely headed in the right direction.

The year was over, and I decided to stick around for the summer session just to get a jump on some of the prerequisite courses that I didn't cover in the fall or spring sessions. The summer session was extremely different than the others. I was so used to the stampede of students throughout the year that it was quite underwhelming to see how drastically different it was in the June and July months. But it was precisely what I needed to grow up. I spent more time with faculty members than ever before. I built relationships with people who became my mentors and ultimately held me accountable for my endeavors, especially being on track to graduate in a few years. The tough love and the reality checks over the summer months set the tone going into my sophomore year.

When my sophomore year began, I volunteered to be a Peer Advisor for the incoming freshmen. Since I wasn't the newbie anymore, I had just enough experience to help the freshmen get a glimpse of what to expect in the coming months. During the same time, my fraternity was gearing up for the first step show of the year during freshman week. I always looked forward to that. Talk about an ego boost; step shows gave you that campus celebrity spotlight. There was nothing like that 15 minutes of fame where everyone is cheering and screaming your name. I earned some step-team experience from high school and was part of the Sigma Beta Club as a teenager; needless to say, I was pretty good at stepping and party hops. Every opportunity I could, if there was music on or with a few of my fraternity brothers, we had to show out. Every one of those moments felt like a competition, and I refused to lose. For that entire year, it felt like most of my focus was geared towards my fraternity which taught me the vital lesson of brotherhood. It was a dope feeling stepping out and being with my guys everywhere. We always were there for one another.

The junior year rolled around, and at this point, I'm kind of a big deal on campus. Being involved in so many activities and organizations, I was one of the guys to get to know. That same year, I had one frat brother involved in the Student Government Association, and he was President of the PanHellenic Council on campus. He was very influential in making things happen on campus. The issue was that he was a senior. Once he graduated, our organization (Phi Beta Sigma, Inc.) would be unrepresented as a seat holder/decision-maker in those positions. I recognized this late in the game when students had already begun the campaign process to be elected for the following year. This is where my freshman year friend, Calvin Williams, Jr, became a game-changer. Even though he was a member of Alpha Phi Alpha, Fraternity, Inc. He was still my brother and close friend. He just so happened to be campaigning to be President of the Student Government Association. I reached out to him and expressed my interest in being Vice President of External Affairs (VPEA). This position had a hand on the most significant social events like Homecoming and Aggie Fest in the spring. I had no clue what I was signing up for, but Calvin looked out. He basically walked me through the campaigning registration process and even introduced me to my campaign manager, Phyllis Robinson. This woman played no games when it came to our campaign. It was like a boxing coach to a boxer. So many late nights drilling on student government concerns and developing speeches, I thought my head was going to explode. Calvin and Phyllis ensured I was on point, from speaking in debates to going door to door through dorms.

The day finally came for ballot boxes to open and close, and I was nervous. So much time and hard work were put in to make this happen. Finally, in the late hours, we got the results. Head down and eyes closed, I heard the names Calvin Williams, Jr. and James Woodert as President and Vice President of SGA. We really did it! I was relieved and anxious at the same time. Yes, I won; however, what did I actually just sign up for? I guess my senior year would be one for the books.

Senior year … what a ride this was! Although I was SGA Vice President, I still thrived in my fraternity. Professionally, I started a party promotion group with my frat brother Danjon Meredith, and I became the lead male singer of a local popular band, Beautiful Experience. Life played out exactly how I wanted it to be, and I felt complete in my life. I was thankful to have stayed focused on doing everything I could imagine during my time at A&T. Those years really set the tone for the rest of my life. I think the biggest lesson I learned was to try everything and see what sticks. This really helped mold my character. So again, I say, if I had to describe my experience at A&T in one word, it would be "fulfilling."

About James Woodert, III

My career in Aviation began in Washington, DC with Human Solutions, Inc. as a Recruiter in the Human Resources Department for the Air traffic Control Sector. I accumulated more experience in my transition into a Program Analyst position for the Federal Aviation Administration. To further my experience, I joined a non-profit, Aviation Youth Mentorship Program, to assist young minority students with getting their pilot's license. As a board member of AYMP, I am passionate about aviation and pilot training. I fully appreciate the power of aviation literacy and aerospace education and feel blessed to have the opportunity to educate and help shape clients' lives.

I am originally from Fayetteville, NC but I currently reside in Washington, DC and enjoy music, traveling, exercising, and spending time at the beach with my wonderful nieces and nephews.

DR. RAUSHANNAH JOHNSON-VERWAYNE

Creating a Legacy as a First-Generation Scholar
Dr. Raushannah Johnson-Verwayne

Growing up, the constant theme was to survive. It was the only mindset that I knew. Not only was the theme to survive but the nickname for my city was "Bad News" [Newport News, VA]. How ironic. I was surrounded by struggle and engulfed by hopelessness and mediocrity. Much of this pervasive mediocrity crept into my home and permeated our atmosphere. I was an excellent student; academics was my safe space. In spite of my environment, I was celebrated and encouraged for being "the smart kid" and my family knew that I was destined for more. Unfortunately, "more" was a mystery.

I left home at eighteen and went to North Carolina A&T State University. I had never heard of A&T. As a first-generation college student, everything was new to me and finding my way was a major all in itself. I majored in psychology and excelled. I can't help but think about the grace that was afforded to me. I knew I wanted to pursue graduate school and my faculty advisors at A&T became like family and pointed me in the right direction. Early on, I had a desire to become a psychologist. It was a spiritual gift that I had to walk into and felt confident that I could do the work even in highly competitive environments. What many people don't realize is that First Gen students face challenges that are unique. Statistics show that many First Gen students do not succeed in higher education for social and economic reasons. Many First Gen students have excelled academically, yet a common factor these students share is a lack of knowledge about how college works and feel overwhelmed early on. One reason for this is that a lot of First Gen students never visit the campus before enrolling. So, they have an uphill battle learning the ropes and are afraid to ask for help from professors and others. On top of that, First Gen students who are not enrolled in a HBCU, have to constantly deal with microaggressions and racial prejudice from the "elitist" student body. These daily behaviors by others may make First Gen students feel isolated and result in low self-esteem. Attending A&T was a protective factor for me.

I graduated Summa Cum Laude, was accepted into a doctorate clinical psychology program and here I am. Today, as a licensed clinical psychologist, author, entrepreneur, docuseries expert, and community advocate, my confidence and the "I can do anything and do it well" mindset is evidence of my NC A&T experience.

Aggie Pride is integrated into my everyday life through fundraising, donating, and in the future, adding the University as a beneficiary. My two children are already naturally Aggies, and I am proud to be the catalyst for generations of greatness.

About Dr. Raushannah Johnson-Verwayne

Dr. Raushannah Johnson-Verwayne, also known as "Dr. RJ" is a licensed clinical psychologist and the founder of Standard of Care Psychological Services, in Atlanta, GA. Dr. RJ integrates self-care with education of the brain and body connection and explains neuroscience in a relatable manner. Whether it's speaking at a women's conference, hosting a corporate retreat, or attending a grassroots community service event, Dr. RJ is passionate about wellness and self-care. Her latest endeavor focuses on helping black women executives and physicians eliminate burnout, anxiety, and stress.

Dr. RJ is the "go-to" professional for any and all topics pertaining to mental health. She has appeared as the expert psychologist on the Lifetime series Killer Kids, Oxygen Network series Snapped: Behind Bars, and on several episodes of the docu-crime series For My Man on TV One. She is the host of Wellness Wednesday for KPRS Hot 103 Jamz in Kansas City, and has authored several blogs and articles for a variety of publications.

As an African-American woman, Dr. RJ recognizes the unique impact of stress on her demographic. Author of the number one new release in clinical psychology, *Stress, Lies and Vacancy: The Self Care Guide to Refill Your Empty Vessel* and of the recently published book, *Overwhelmed: The Self-Care Guide for College Students*, Dr. RJ's experiences and transparency provides self-help for people of color to reduce common stressors in their lives that have long term effects on the body and brain. Dr. RJ's favorite quote is "Self-care isn't selfish. You can't serve from an empty vessel".

KENTAE & ARNITA MORRIS

A Whole New World
Kentae & Arnita Morris

Through Kentae's Lens

The youngest of five children, I was born and raised in Grimesland, North Carolina. Yes, I know; it sounds like it is in the backwoods somewhere...it is. Unlike kids today, I was glad to go outside and play, build clubhouses, drink from the water hose, and walk through the woods. My father and most of my siblings went to the military after high school. After the military, my father worked for a pharmaceutical company, and my mother was a housewife. Growing up, I liked school, but I didn't really have any expectations beyond high school. Where I'm from, it was not pushed to further your education. The main goal was to graduate from high school. That, in itself, was an accomplishment. So, I had no plans on going to college and definitely didn't know what an HBCU was. It wasn't until halfway through my senior year that I decided I would go. I only applied to one school, North Carolina Agricultural & Technical State University (A&T). I remember my father's answer when the financial adviser came to our house and asked how much he had put away for my college fund. He shook his head and said, "Zero." I was crushed, thinking I would be stuck at home, but I was able to pay for college the way most people did... grants and loans. Coming from a home with older-aged parents, I didn't get to do much traveling or getting out, so when I got to A&T, my mind was blown.

In August 1999, my brother and his wife dropped me off on campus and helped me move into my dormitory (Scott Hall B). My roommate was my cousin. We graduated from high school together and requested to be roommates, so I already knew at least one person there. The first few weeks were overly stimulating for me. There was so much going on that I had not been previously exposed to. I immediately immersed myself in the culture. I can remember the band marching through the yard every evening practicing. The "strip" was packed with students all day, knowing they needed to be in class. And all the organizations being active and representing. My friends and I would meet up every day and eat at Williams Cafeteria (The Caf) or the "Annex" when the Caf was being renovated. Two of the organizations I joined as a freshman were the Student Union Advisory Board (SUAB) and the Aggie Live Wires. Through these organizations, I was able to come up with programs for the student body and showcase what Aggie Pride is. Because of my involvement in those organizations, I met new people who caused me to join the National Society of Black Engineers (NSBE) in 2000. I was on the NSBE step team for several years, showcasing at regional, national, and homecoming step shows.

With NSBE, I was allowed to travel all over the United States, network with Fortune 500 companies, interact with celebrities and see some amazing things. In Fall 2001, I became a member of Alpha Phi Omega National Coed Service Fraternity. The principles of this organization are leadership, friendship, and service. This organization really provided me with an outlet to lead and serve others. It is for that reason that I decided to run for an elected position in NSBE. In 2002, I was elected as the Vice President, and in 2003, I was elected as the President. These positions were very respected and influential, as NSBE was one of the largest organizations on campus at the time. Everything that I did up until this point would prepare me for the next milestone in my life. In Spring 2003, I pledged the best chapter and fraternity on this side of glory (lol), the Beta Epsilon chapter of Alpha Phi Alpha Fraternity, Incorporated.

I would like to thank my Dean and ADPs for their wise choice of pledgees. I lucked out with getting put with such a great group of brothers. I make it a goal to see and get with these guys for a trip at least once every year. Lifelong bonds were formed through Beta Epsilon. After I pledged, most of my time was split between Alpha and NSBE, with a sprinkle of classes and homework here and there. I took a few semesters off due to financial hardship and the passing of my father. I graduated in the Spring of 2006. I was just a few years off target, but I made it.

In my experience at A&T, I found that the faculty and staff genuinely cared. It was never about a paycheck or tenure for them; they just wanted us to try hard and succeed. The people that I met at A&T have genuinely become lifelong friends and family. My advice to anyone that is struggling to fit in is "be yourself." You can't fake it all your life, so you might as well be who you are. I've always been about selfless service and being a part of something bigger than myself. Therefore, those are the types of things and people I gravitated towards. My father always said, "Don't give up, give out." I gave so much of myself and will continue to do everything that encompasses that principle because I can.

Arnita's Experience

Growing up in Philadelphia, my mom always encouraged me to see the world. My mom and dad worked hard to provide for me. My family taught me the importance of education, hard work, and entrepreneurship. Picking a college was a difficult task; however, I was intrigued by the ideas of HBCUs. It would be a contrast to my melting pot experience at Central High School. So to ensure I was making the right choice, I prayed that my acceptance letter would come on my birthday. On January 10, 2003, my birthday, my acceptance letter came from A&T. I had never set foot on this campus, but I knew it was God's will. He always sends sweet whispers to confirm you are on His path.

Going to A&T was one of the best decisions I made. I made lifelong friends that have become my family. The most important thing I learned during college was how to follow, advocate for others and lead. As a freshman and sophomore at A&T, I served in the Senate. I learned so much about writing legislation, building relationships with people, and leading. As a sophomore, I worked with the Student Government Association (SGA) in creating a conference for HBCU leaders on campus called the HBCU Think Tank. Next, I went on to run for Vice President of Internal Affairs, and I won. So, from 2005-2006, I led the Senate and worked with other SGAs across the state with an organization called the Association of Student Governments. I continued my journey of leadership the following year by serving as the 2006-2007 SGA president. My administration successfully passed the Mr. A&T and Court legislation to have our first Campus King next year. In addition, we worked with the International Civil Rights Museum to fundraise for their opening. It was a year full of ups and downs. After focusing so much on leading, my grades dropped, and anxiety set in. For the first time in my life, I went to therapy, which helped me feel much more balanced. Instead of burying my pain, I was working through it. At the end of my senior year, I learned that if you don't take care of yourself first, you won't be able to maintain anything with excellence. My SGA advisors were so instrumental in supporting me and making me the leader I am today. I will always be indebted to dear A&T for teaching me so many lessons and supporting me.

How We Met

We were already acquainted with each other through our leadership roles on the yard. In the summer of 2006, a mutual friend invited us to lunch at The Caf. Over lunch, we discussed what plans she had for A&T and what she wanted to accomplish while in office. Neither of us was looking for a relationship, but we stayed in contact. Eventually, the phone calls and texts turned into us dating and finally putting a title on it. Now, here we are, fifteen years and three kids later, still kicking it.

Future Generations

When our kids grow up, we want them to experience the joy of attending an HBCU. The pride that we have in A&T, the confidence instilled in us, and the connections to other graduates is something we want them to experience. It was indeed a priceless experience that helped to make us into the people we are today. We continue to donate and give back to A&T to continue to be around for our children and others to experience its legacy.

About Kentae & Arnita Morris

Kentae and Arnita Morris are both proud graduates of North Carolina Agricultural and Technical State University. Kentae graduated with a Bachelor of Arts degree in Liberal Studies (2006) and Arnita graduated with a Bachelor of Science degree in Business Administration with a concentration in management (2007). While attending, they were very active on campus and in their organizations. Kentae served as the 2002-2003 Vice President and 2003-2004 President of the National Society of Black Engineers as well as various positions in other organizations. Arnita served on the Senate and was the 2005-2006 Vice President of Internal Affairs and 2006-2007 Student Government Association President. They are both members of the divine nine. Kentae, being a member of Alpha Phi Alpha Fraternity, Incorporated (2003) and Arnita, a member of Delta Sigma Theta Sorority, Incorporated (2008). Kentae went on to earn a Master of Business Administration degree from the University of Phoenix (2016). Arnita also sought higher education, earning a Master of Education degree in Middle Grades Math from Western Governor's University (2012). They are the proud parents of three beautiful and amazing children; Kaleb, Malaysia, and Addison. They are truly lifelong servant-leaders. Currently, Kentae serves in the United States Marine Corps as the Chief Maintenance Supervisor for Ground Electronics and Communication Systems aboard Marine Corps Air Station Cherry Point. Arnita is an 8th grade Middle School Math teacher at H. J. Macdonald Middle School in New Bern, NC, where she has led the Math department since 2018. She is also the 2021 Craven County Schools Teacher of the Year. They continue to serve the community and country in hopes that something they say or do will impact someone in a positive way.

BENJAMIN ROBINSON

Aggie Born and Aggie Bred
Benjamin Robinson

I was raised by proud HBCU graduates who taught me the importance of education. While I grew up attending JSCU homecomings and The Aggie Eagle Classic at Carter Finley Stadium in Raleigh, North Carolina, I had no intention to attend those schools myself. Long before graduating from Southeast Raleigh High School in 2005, I decided that college wasn't for me. I wasn't the best student in high school, and I just did what I was told to do. I didn't know what I actually wanted to do or who I wanted to be in life.

My parents encouraged me to apply to college anyway, preferably an HBCU in North Carolina because they believed in an HBCU education. As a result, I was accepted into three HBCUs: Johnson C. Smith University, North Carolina Central State University, and North Carolina Agricultural State University.

I knew that people who attended North Carolina A&T were all very proud to be Aggies and carried themselves differently. I was unsure what made them this way, but everyone had the same pride-filled reaction whenever you mentioned the school. Broadcast Production was a new interest at the time, and I was curious to figure out if it was a short-lived hobby or a real passion. So, even though I didn't know much about North Carolina A&T or what I would study in school, I eventually decided to enroll there because of its culture and journalism program.

There were so many lessons I learned throughout my time at the University. I cannot begin to tell you how much the staff and facility helped nurture and groom me into the man I am today, with respect to my parents. Black women played a pivotal role in my growth at the University. Dr. Marrissa R. Dick, a secretary for the Journalism and Mass Communication Department, became my unofficial counselor and remained a trusted mentor until I graduated. She told me which professors and classes to take and how I should carry myself. I know I would have not made it to graduation if it wasn't for her. There were also the incredible women whom I worked with at the Colleges of Arts and Sciences. That entire office gave me employment and trusted me with so many jobs.

Moreover, the office as a whole adopted me. They would provide food for me if I was hungry. They made sure I understood how to be professional at work and helped me any way they could. After college, I still received help from women like Dr. Teresa Style. She personally wrote a letter for me to attend my graduate program at Elon University. She was also someone who I could ask for advice and mentorship. There are many incredible women to name, but I have to talk about the late great Deirdre Cherie "D Cherie" Lofton. D Cherie was WFAA award-winning program director and music director. She gave me the opportunity to work with the radio station whenever she had major artists come through. D Cherie believed in my talent and was always there to support me. When I applied to graduate school, she also wrote me a recommendation letter, and I am forever grateful to her. These women did not have to help me, but they did. They did not receive any extra pay or credit. I am forever indebted to them for setting me up for success in my life and career.

I still remember the first time I heard the phrase "Aggie Pride!" Aggie Pride is an acronym that stands for "Achieving Great Goals in Everything – Producing Renowned Individuals Dedicated to Excellence." People would say this all around the North Carolina A&T campus. At first, I did not believe it was a real thing. I thought these people were absolutely crazy, and I assumed the phrase was just university propaganda that worked. Little did I know it was more than an acronym; it was a way of life. Throughout my time at the university, friends turned into family. This was extremely transparent for me when my younger brother attended the school my senior year. I have always been my brother's keeper but never had to worry about him at school. My brother told me that everyone was always showing him love (maybe too much love at times) on campus. People would constantly tell him, "You're Ben's little brother!" Freshman year tends to be an adjustment for most people, but it was easy for my brother. He told me people would give him rides, offer him food, and even free drinks! As an older sibling, I was happy and proud other students received my brother very well. My brother went on to become Freshman and Sophomore Class President, followed by Vice President of External Affairs and finally, Student Body President. These constant acts of love and support toward him can only be described as Aggie Pride.

There is so much more I can say about the university. I would walk around campus smiling because I could not believe I attended this great school. The university became my safe space, a place where I could nourish and grow with beautiful black minds as the product of great history. Attending the university has been one of the greatest honors I have ever had. The only experience more significant than that is being an alum of the school. We are a proud group and take care of one another. I am honored to walk the same dorms as the four men who walked into Woolworth on February 1st and helped start the Civil Rights Sit-ins. I'm proud I have attended the largest public HBCU in the nation. I would recommend that any high school student interested in college take a serious look at North Carolina A&T University. This is a safe place to grow and learn from your mistakes. In Aggieland, you can dream and achieve your goals. I am a true Aggie and proud of it. Aggie Born and Aggie Bred, and when I die, I'll be Aggie Dead!

About Benjamin Robinson

Benjamin M. Robinson is a native of Raleigh, North Carolina. He is a proud graduate of North Carolina A&T State University with a degree in Journalism and Mass Communication. Benjamin also has a Master's in Interactive Media from Elon University. He is currently a visual storyteller and digital designer for HKS Inc., the second-largest architecture firm in the United States. He is a storyteller who takes personal responsibility to document today's culture through film and uses various tools like social media to inform people. He creates experiences that attract and engage audiences' attention through storytelling. Good storytelling can help solve problems and share ideas by connecting people with information in the right context. Asking questions establishing a body of knowledge both about the audience and client allows him to craft emotional moments through image, web, and video. Benjamin was previously a visual journalist for The Dallas Morning News. He has covered several notable new stories including the Botham Jean and Jordan Edwards cases. He has also captured everything from U.S Presidents to Dallas Cowboys games.

DR. ANDREW HEADD

Blessed and Highly Favored
Dr. Andrew Headd

I grew up in a very structured household, where both parents were present. My dad served in the US Army and later became a pastor. My mother worked at the Military Entrance Processing Command (MEPS). From a young age, I saw my parents work, raise a family, and be involved in the community while continuing their education. My dad ultimately earned his Ph.D. Being raised in a military household as a preacher's kid, I developed a certain mindset that would ultimately prepare me for adulthood. I understood the value of working hard, self-discipline, and perseverance. As I reflect, I was very blessed because I didn't have to look any further than the other side of the dinner table for a role model.

Most of my elementary and middle school years were spent in Montgomery, Alabama. Although I lived within a 10-mile radius from Alabama State University and spent countless weekends at Tuskegee University, when my dad worked there, I decided that I would attend Auburn University. When I was in middle school, I decided to become a dentist when I got older.

In 1997, as I was preparing for my first year in high school, my dad was called to pastor a church in Smithfield, NC. My world was rocked because I was going to leave the place that I had lived the longest, and I was going to leave my friends. Growing up in a military household, we moved a little more than the average family. My birthplace is Ackerman, MS. When my dad joined the Army, we moved to Alexandria, VA; Ft. Buchanan, PR; then Montgomery, AL - all before I turned eight years old! When it was time to move to North Carolina, my parents allowed me to stay and live with a neighbor. I attended Sidney Lanier High School. Although I appreciated staying in Montgomery, my grades began to slip; and I eventually got in a bit of trouble. My parents withdrew me, and I moved to North Carolina the week of Thanksgiving break.

When I got to North Carolina and began to attend school, I was in a bit of a cultural shock. I went to a very diverse school, which was very different for me. The students who looked like me were involved in church, and it was 'cool' to get good grades. For years, I intentionally made average grades. I was forced to go to church on Wednesday, Saturday, and Sunday. Here, the students sang gospel songs in gym class and joined the gospel choir at school. My dad's church, First Missionary Baptist Church of Smithfield, was composed of members who mainly attended Historically Black Colleges and Universities (HBCU's). There were alumni from North Carolina Central University, Shaw University, St. Augustine College, Tuskegee University, and North Carolina A&T State University. Because of who my parents were, I quickly began to be tapped for social, civic, and service initiatives. I participated in Oratorical Contests, North Carolina Senate Page, North Carolina House Page, a speaker in Dr. Martin Luther King Jr. Day Programs, teen committees with Congressmen, and multiple North Carolina Baptist Association positions. Once I became involved, I began to allow my true self to shine.

Through the exposure I was receiving, I was invited to my first Aggie-Eagle Classic in 1998 by church member, Dr. Phyllis Etheridge (NCCU). Although she was trying to introduce me to NCCU, something about the Blue & Gold Marching Machine ignited my interest. The tailgating, fans, smiles, and the family experience were captured in my mind. However, the family experience reminded me of certain memories from when I was younger. Growing up in Montgomery and watching '*A Different World*,' I saw the Reverend Jessie Jackson. I remember seeing Reverend Jackson wearing a sweater from North Carolina A&T State University.

Once the other members of our church who attended other HBCU's heard about my first experience of the Aggie- Eagle Classic, they quickly began to expose me to their universities. However, still in my mind, my first college choice was Auburn University.

I was introduced to the trumpet when I was in the sixth grade. Mr. Alexander was my band teacher at Cloverdale Middle School -Montgomery. Like any other boy, I didn't want to play the trumpet. I wanted to play the drums. I hated it so much that I did everything I could to not have to play. It felt like Mr. Alexander called my mom every day. What I didn't know was that when I moved to North Carolina, there would be a man who lived down the street from me who also played the trumpet. Deacon John 'Doc' Windley went to North Carolina A&T SU (C/O 1957). Deacon Windley formed a band at our church, and I was his lead trumpet player. After school, I would walk to Deacon Windley's home, and we would practice playing.

Along with Deacon Windley, there was another Aggie that I had the opportunity to meet. Deacon William Clayton (C/O 1963) sat me down after church many times to share his love for North Carolina A&T. When it was time to apply for college, I decided to go on an official visit to North Carolina A&T SU. I asked Deacon Windley and Deacon Clayton if they would take me. That may have been the greatest honor for them. Together, we drove the 90 miles to Greensboro. When I took my first step on the campus, I immediately knew that this was where I belonged! I applied and was accepted.

My mom took me to Freshman Orientation. We drove around Greensboro for hours, looking for a Walmart, and we were just as lost as could be on Hwy 29 and Wendover. This was before Waze, so we had to print our directions from MapQuest. At orientation, I remember hearing the leaders give us the charge during the General Assembly: "Look to your left. Look to your right. One of you will not be back next semester."

I immediately thought back to my high school experience in Alabama; when my grades dropped, I got into trouble, and I had to go 'home.' In my mind, I said it wouldn't be me! I knew I had what it took to make it here. To become a dentist, I started my freshman year (2001) as a biology major. Later, I was notified that I was awarded the Hercules Scholarship from the Tom Joyner Morning Show. My mom had applied for this scholarship since she listened to the Tom Joyner Morning Show every morning.

My freshman year, I was assigned to the Scott B dormitory. Then, I lived in the Aggie Inn during my sophomore year. Because of my major and the words that I heard during orientation, I endured countless overnight stays in the Bluford Library. Every day when I walked into the library, I would ask the security guard how he was doing. His response was always, "Blessed and highly favored." I ate in the trailer (café) every day, endured the flooding of my dorm room, and witnessed September 11th.

After a year as a biology major, I changed my major to mathematics. I didn't have a valid reason. I just did it. This move is what I believe placed me on the right track for determining my true purpose in life. One day during physics class, this young lady was sitting two rows in front of me. There was something about her that intrigued me, though I was too nervous to talk to her. On Friday nights, I would go bowling with my freshman roommate and some of his friends in his major (IE). Maybe a year later, one night when we were out bowling, here walks in this young lady from my physics class. She spoke to everyone in our party, except me. Though nervous still, I boldly walked up to her and introduced myself. With that conversation, we became friends, started dating, going to church together, and eventually would marry in 2008 and start a family together.

In the Spring of 2005, I was initiated into the Alpha Nu Chapter of Kappa Alpha Psi Fraternity, Inc. Two months later, I graduated. But I didn't leave Greensboro just yet. I began my first year of teaching at Hairston Middle School. Fast-forward 16 years, I serve in one of the best school districts in the nation, Gwinnett County Public Schools (GCPS), a two-time winner of The Broad Prize. I mentor young African American males through a program I started, The Gentlemen's Society.

Due to my strong family upbringing, God's blessings abound in my life. I've found success in living out His purpose for my life, educating and supporting our youth, the future of our nation. Moving from Alabama to North Carolina removed me from negativity and allowed me to attend North Carolina A&T State University. His favor allowed me to meet my kind and loving wife and have the ability to provide for my own family and raise God-fearing children. I'm excited about living the next steps of my life!

About Dr. Andrew C. Headd

Dr. Andrew C. Headd currently serves as a high school administrator in Georgia's largest school district, Gwinnett County Public Schools. He has been involved in education for the last 16 years, serving in various roles. His professional career began in 2005, when he accepted his first teaching position at Hairston Middle School in Greensboro, NC as a 6th Grade Math Teacher. Additionally, he has served as a 6th Grade Math and Science teacher at Brogden Middle School (Durham, NC), Academic Advisor with the Educational Talent Search Program at Fayetteville State University (Fayetteville, NC), Math Professor at Johnston Community College (Smithfield, NC), Learning Specialist at North Carolina State University (Raleigh, NC), and Administrative Intern at Jackson Central-Merry High School (Jackson, TN).

In 2016, Dr. Headd started a male mentoring club at Grayson High School. *'The Gentlemen's Society'* was created to promote leadership, academics, college/career readiness, and interpersonal development for a select group of male students. This select group of intelligent, talented, and respectful young men participate in bi-monthly leadership sessions that focus on learning the positive attributes of leadership, college and career goal-setting initiatives, resume building, interviewing, and projects that promote positive school culture.

Dr. Headd is a native of Louisville, MS. Growing up in a military household, he also spent some years in Alexandria, VA; Ft. Buchanan, Puerto Rico; Montgomery, AL; and Smithfield, NC. Dr. Headd received his Bachelor of Science in Mathematics from North Carolina Agricultural & Technical State University in 2005. He also holds a Masters' degree in Educational Management and an Educational Specialist degree in School Leadership. In 2017, he received his Doctor of Education degree in Educational Leadership from Clark-Atlanta University.

Dr. Headd is a Spring 2005 Initiate into the Alpha Nu Chapter of Kappa Alpha Psi Fraternity, Inc. He is married to Alishia (Herndon) Headd, who is also an alumnus of North Carolina A&T State University. Mrs. Alishia has a B.S. in Industrial & Systems Engineering, and is a Spring 2004 Initiate into the Alpha Phi Chapter of Alpha Kappa Alpha Sorority, Inc. Together, they have two beautiful children: Aubrey and Andrew (AJ) Headd and they currently live in Smyrna, GA.

JUSTIN JORRELL MOORE

They Are, Who I Am
Justin Jorrell Moore

I have all the stories! I went to A&T and I did all you could do! I went to all my classes and I went to all the parties. I was at every football game and every basketball game. The House Party, The Pre-Game, The Day Party, The Club, and The After Party. In *all* the step shows. In the cafe food fight. In the Aggie Suites during a snowstorm black out. At the Verge vs. Couture fashion shows. At the Gospel Choir concerts. I was in The Blue and Gold Marching Machine (BGMM), the Jazz band, the Pep band, and the Chamber Singers. I was The Scarecrow in the Theater Department's production of The Wiz. I was throwing K's with KKPsi and hoppin' with the Ques! I did the Aggie Lean as Drum Major for the BGMM. I went to summer school and graduated Cum Laude. **I have all the stories.** Some of them will never be spoken of again or only in private with the people who were in that room; some are my favorite thoughts that I replay in my mind and many of these stories have left an incredible lasting effect on me and the way I live my life. I will do my best to share one with you in the next 1500 words. Pray for me.

It was in April, 2009. I remember because 2008-09 was one of the most impactful years of my life. I was in a whirlwind of emotions and extremes of complete joy and hope along with depression and anxiety. I had become a brother of the Mu Psi Chapter of Omega Psi Phi, the first Black President had just been elected, I had just graduated, and my brother, Dennis S. Hayle, had recently been a victim of gun violence. In the midst of all of this was a moment of clarity; something caught my eye. I saw a flyer for auditions for "The Wiz" the musical. Now when I was a child, "The Wiz" was my favorite movie! I would come home from middle school and put that tape in the VCR and blast that joint, singing every song full voice until someone in my family would make it home. I was also a child performer, so, ever since then, I said to myself, I was going to be the Scarecrow! When I saw the flyer, all of those childhood thoughts flowed through my mind, and I knew that I had to do this - it was meant for me. I could feel it.

Now, even though I'm seeing this for the first time, the audition is TODAY! If I'm going to do this, it has to happen now. What am I going to sing? What are they going to ask me? I don't know the answer to any of these questions, but I just had to go. At the same time I am currently the hop master for da bruhs and the Aggie Fest step show is coming up so we have practice all the time. Being a neo in Omega Psi Phi is super fun but no walk in the park with a very thin line for error. Da bruhs will take all your time, and I was obliged to give it. But this was different; it was "The Wiz!" So I had to do a power play. I started hop practice, thankfully this squad was seasoned bruhs, and with Kwame Molden, the previous hop master, still in the ranks I knew that we were good. I don't remember how I was able to get out of that room for the audition, but I'm sure it wasn't me telling the full truth. I sprinted across the quad to the New Classroom building, (it's not "new" by this point, just still without a real name) and I ran in late and loudly to the audition for the musical. It's an open audition… meaning everyone gets to watch everyone's audition, and in walks me, this out of breath sweaty guy in a Q-Dawg purple shirt with the sleeves cut off and basketball shorts with gold boots! Everyone's face was ready for the embarrassment that had to follow whatever this guy was going to do. "What will you be singing?", says the pianist. "What are you going to sing?", I thought, I probably should have thought about that before this moment." My best friend D'Javon popped into my mind and I sang the song he always told me to sing, "Lately" by Stevie Wonder. Praise God the pianist already knew it because I was completely unprepared. After the song everyone's eyes were in complete shock, this nasty dog just crushed that piece. Me and my gold boots sat back down for the rest of the audition.

Next is the dancing part of the audition, the others were putting on shoes made for dance, and I got on these gold combat boots. I know they thought I was crazy, but coming from marching band, boots and dancing are second nature to me. I'm the Drum Major! So, my last five years of late nights with the marching band learning this weeks' new breakdown, had me ready for this moment. I felt really good about what had just happened.

Sprinting back across the quad to hop practice, I was so happy that I had gone to the audition, if only to fulfill a childhood desire. Back with da bruhs it's on and poppin', no one knows that I just dipped out to hit an audition for a musical, and outside of my line brothers I was going to leave it that way. We had a step show to go probably not win, the Ques don't care about your winning, we know who we are and we know that you love it.

A few days later… the cast list is posted, beside The Scarecrow is my name. I instantly see myself on stage singing "You Can't Win" from the movie, even though it's not in the stage play! I had no clue what I was walking into, and Aggie Fest was going to be on the same day as the first weekend of the play, so I had to make a choice. It was very hard to tell my bruhs that I needed to step down from the show, bruhs were not pleased, and I knew it and understood, but I had their blessing.

Performing in Paul Robeson Theatre under Dr. Daye and Prof. Baldwin-Bradby was a game changer. There is nothing like being on the 50-yard line with all eyes on you doing the Aggie Lean while the stadium of the Greatest Homecoming On Earth screams "AGGIE PRIDE" at you during half time, nothing like that. It was a whole new adoration in its own right; I found an unexplored part of myself on that stage. Come to find out, my father also performed on that stage while he was in college at UNCG. I was also able to build a whole new family in a new realm of the campus that I had never been a part of. I won an Obie Award for "Best Performance" from the Theater Department; I am the first non-theater major to be awarded that honor. Even my line brothers, who I had abandoned at the Aggie Fest step show, saw the play and knew that I had to make that choice. With line names like Devon M*I*Zes and ConduQtor, it was obvious that I belonged on stage.

I am extremely blessed. That was the beginning of my career as an Actor, where I am now professionally performing in New York City theaters. Those moments are what groomed, molded, nurtured, and built the person that I am today. I've been an Aggie my whole life, and like many others, it was the only university I even considered in high school. I would have been successful no matter what school I decided to attend, but it was God's will for me to be successful at A&T. I know that if you made it to my chapter in this book, you can already tell that the Aggies who were with me were all successful, powerful, abundant, strong and lively individuals. They are who I am. That's what Aggie Pride stands for. I carry it into every room I walk in and every hand I shake.

"... And when I die, I'll be Aggie dead."

About Justin Jorrell Moore

Justin Jorrell Moore is an Aggie. Born and Bred. The son of a Preacher and a Teacher, Justin was born in Greensboro and raised in Charlotte, North Carolina. He received his Bachelors of Science in Music Education with the Alto Saxophone as his principal instrument. For five years, Justin was fully dedicated to A&T's marching band, the Blue and Gold Marching Machine; two of those years were spent as the Drum Major for the band. Justin also played the Tenor Sax in the University Jazz band under the leadership of Dr. Henry and Prof. Moffett and the Symphonic band directed by Dr. Ruff. He was in the University Chamber Choir, singing first tenor, led by Prof. Trice. Justin is a proud brother of Iota Zeta chapter of Kappa Kappa Psi National Honorary Band Fraternity Inc. and the Mu Psi Chapter of Omega Psi Phi Fraternity Inc. His passion for performing and music led him into the family of A&T's Theater Dep. where he was cast in his first musical as The Scarecrow in The Wiz directed by Prof. Donna Baldwin-Bradby on the Paul Robeson Theater stage on campus. It is here that Justin found where he would focus his attention and goals. Returning to Charlotte after graduating, Justin taught K-5 music at Nathaniel Alexander Elementary and Hidden Valley Elementary schools simultaneously, while joining the theatre production family, OnQ Productions. During this time, Justin was given the space to grow as an actor in plays like Funny House of a Negro, The Coloured Museum and the musicals The Civil War and Floyd Collins. Now, after 7 years in New York City, Justin has been using all his tools that were cultivated and groomed while at NC A&T SU. He has performed professionally as an actor with many different theater groups throughout the City and surrounding area, also a premier Master of Ceremonies for live events like music festivals, concerts, galas, and fund raisers. Justin Jorrell is so thankful and grateful for each and every moment lived at A&T; every smiley wipe, every 8 o'clock class, every Aggie Lean, every bark, every pre-game and every black party. Thank you Supreme Source. Thank You A&T. Thank You Dennis Hayle.

APRIL J. GARRETT, MS

A HBCU Legacy of an Aggie
April J. Garrett, MS

Attending Historically Black Colleges and Universities was always a big thing in my family. It was instilled in me that the confidence and pride that I would gain would be one of the best times of my life that could not be matched at any other school. My parents, both grandmothers, aunts, uncles, and cousins had all attended one. The impressions that Bethune Cookman University, Florida Agriculture & Mechanical University, and Howard University left on my family members were powerful. So, I knew that I was going to following in their footsteps and attend an HBCU.

Growing up in Miami, Florida, there was a heavy presence of HBCU alumni; however, there were not many ways to experiences life on the campus. So, my parents would take my sister and me to events that showcased that "black college experience." We went to HBCU football games, battle of the bands, and step shows in hopes of giving us a glimpse of what it was like.

My father, Mr. Willie C. Garrett, class of 1967, attained his bachelor's degree from North Carolina Agricultural and Technical State University. As a little girl, every year, my family traveled to Greensboro to attend Homecoming. Chanting "Aggie Pride" at those icy cold Homecoming football games, seeing my dad play the trumpet in the Alumni band, cheering along with the cheerleaders, and dancing to the sounds of the horns that filled the air from the band were moments I treasured. My mom, sister, and I would listen to stories from my dad and his buddies on their experiences as members of The Blue and Gold Marching Machine. They were always happy to return and participate in the Alumni band each year and show they "still had it" while high stepping and twirling their instruments.

In August of 1988, just before I went to fifth grade, my sister Mrs. Jessica Garrett Modkins, class of 1992, became a freshman at A&T. Moving into her dorm room at Curtis Hall was the start of her college experience. As years went by, she would call me and show me pictures of her life as an Aggie. She talked about hanging out at the Student Union and reporting the news on the school's radio station WNAA. She even taught me how to model like she did in Mo'del Unique. The family's annual homecoming trip took on a different perspective while my sister attended A&T. I was able to see the campus from my big sisters' point of view. It was AWESOME! All of the black excellence around me was mind-blowing and inspiring.

Years later, as I matriculated through high school, I began to figure out it was time for my own HBCU path. In my junior year, I participated in a college tour that traveled along the East Coast to visit several HBCU's. This tour opened my eyes to other colleges that had great things to offer as well. Although I had many years of that "Old Aggie Spirit," I was not exactly sure that I wanted to go there. Then, during my senior year, my mom Mrs. Patricia Harper Garrett, class of 1967 from Bethune Cookman College, came to my room when I returned home from cheerleading practice and declared I should attend A&T. She knew that I was trying to find which college I would feel like I was at "home" attending. I was surprised she suggested it, but her reasoning made so much sense.

"Since your sister followed in your dads' footsteps, you may as well too," my mother stated. She went on to say, "That way, you two can continue the yearly homecoming trips together with your families like we do now." That simple statement made me remember how much joy I experienced whenever I attended homecomings with my family. I was filled with excitement as I reminisced on all of the stories I heard from my dad and sister. I suddenly realized that the feeling of the joy of homecoming was what I was seeking to have in the college I was going to attend. I knew that I definitely wanted to continue taking those trips and sharing each other's experiences in

Aggieland. I wanted to continue the tradition and the legacy of being an Aggie. Needless to say, the choice was made, the deal was sealed, and I could not wait to become an Aggie.

In the fall of 1996, I became the third Garrett to attend A&T and moved into my dorm room in Vanstory Hall. It was my time to experience all that A&T had to offer me. You could not tell me anything! Do you hear me?! I was fancy-free walking through campus with my roommate, bopping to the cars passing through campus blasting the latest hit CD's. I was now partying at the "Gym Jams," chilling at the Student Union, sitting on the wall in front of the bookstore, and eating at the Café.

I later started to feel homesick; I missed my family. Friends of mine would go home to visit their family on the weekends, and I felt so bad just sitting there in my dorm. A plane ticket to Miami was not the cheapest thing back then. If I participated in something that I enjoyed doing in Miami, I would feel better. I decided to try out for cheerleading, and I made the Junior Varsity Cheerleading squad. I was once again living my best life! Can I get an Aggie Pride? Aggie Pride! Our debut as a squad was at the 1996 Homecoming festivities. There I was, in the same Homecoming Parade that I witnessed my dad participate in for so many years. This time, I joined him as a JV Cheerleader. This was a full-circle moment that I will not ever forget.

As the first semester ended, I quickly realized that I was living my best life a little too much. My grades were nothing like those I earned in high school. I had to pull them from the pits of hell. It was time to focus more on living my best academic life and not just my best social life. I had some academic and personal ups and downs. I changed my major multiple times. I went from Elementary Education to Physical Education; I was trying to figure it out. I finally settled on making my minor in Psychology my major. This was when I began to get into the rhythm of my college life.

I continued to do big things in other areas as well. I participated as a Varsity Cheerleader until I graduated. During that time, my squad and I won the 2000 MEAC Cheerleading Championship. We got rings and all! In the Spring of 2001, I became a member of the Alpha Phi Chapter of Alpha Kappa Alpha Sorority, Inc. This allowed me to be active on campus and in the community outside of the Aggie Cheerleader capacity. We worked on campus and in the community for the good of others. Homecoming 2001 came around, and not only did I have the responsibility of maintaining my grades as a student and participating as Aggie Cheerleader, but I also participated as a member of my chapter's Step Team. We became the 2001 Homecoming Step Show champions.

As my 2002 graduation got closer, I began to see how much I had grown. I was leaving as a stronger young lady than I arrived. A&T had taught me determination. I was prepared for much more than just a career in the Psychology field; I was prepared for whatever life handed me as a proud Aggie woman.

I am so thankful and forever grateful to have had my own experience as an Aggie. I was able to meet people and share experiences that exemplified Black Excellence in my own world. Since graduation, I attained my master's degree in Guidance and Counseling to assist me in helping students live their best lives. In 2021, I am a seasoned School Counselor with over a decade and a half of educational knowledge used to guide the students that I am privileged to help grow toward success. Recently I was recognized as one of *Miami's Top Black Educators* of 2021 by *Legacy Magazine*. It was such an honor to be recognized. I know that my family, experience at A&T, and the woman I have become have made an impression on my students, the community, and ultimately the future. My parents, sister, and I continue to take our yearly Homecoming trip. Now, my sister and I have the opportunity to share these experiences with our children. It came back full circle, and the legacy lives on. I will continue to blaze trails because that's what Aggies do!

About April J. Garrett, MS

"Be an intentional light that shines wisdom and radiates love." April J. Garrett, MS is an accomplished leader and Professional School Counselor with almost two decades of experience in the education field. Born and raised in Miami, FL by a family of Educators, she believed that she was able to make a difference and provide guidance and compassion to push students to their highest potential and support them through their lowest social and emotional problems.

Garrett received her Bachelor's degree in Psychology from North Carolina Agricultural & Technical University in Greensboro, North Carolina. While there, she participated as a Cheerleader and was a member of the Alpha Phi Chapter of Alpha Kappa Alpha Sorority, Inc. Upon graduation, she returned home to Miami and became a teacher. After the first couple of years of teaching, Garrett decided to pursue her true calling, and gain her Master's degree in Guidance and Counseling from St. Thomas University in Miami Gardens, Florida. As a result of her passion towards her students, many have moved on to become college graduates, business owners, and empowered young adults making positive contributions to the world and the community. This impression on the community has led her to be recognized as one of *Miami's Top Black Educators* of 2021 by Miami's *Legacy Magazine*.

Along with her professional career and participating in numerous professional organizations for counseling, Garrett enjoys spending time with her son Jaden, in Jack & Jill of America, Inc., where she serves as Teen Sponsor. She participates on several committees within her beloved Alpha Alpha Beta Omega Chapter of Alpha Kappa Alpha, Inc. She also serves the community as a Founding and Executive Board Member of The Historic Society, a non-profit organization that is dedicated in preserving the rich history of South Florida for generations to come. In her down time, she enjoys creating crafts, listening to music, and spending time with her family and friends in the beautiful Miami sun.

NAKHIA CROSSLEY

A Divinely [Miss]Guided Journey
Nakhia Crossley

I was born and raised in the DMV area, more specifically Northeast Washington D.C. and Prince George's County, Maryland. I am the oldest of three children born from a fierce, single mom with parents who traveled from McComb, Mississippi to live in Washington D.C. when they were eight months pregnant with her. I believe my mother had great expectations for me because she had the same model and expectations from my grandparents; to figure out what you want and when you have figured it out, go get it. There are no limits. She taught me to do the best I can and remain true to myself, even if it means starting over a few times in life. I will always love her for that.

Always a high achiever in school, I knew that attending college was going to be part of my path as a very young girl. However, as a first-generation college graduate, I did not quite know or have someone to emulate to get there. I don't recall doing much research, but I do remember receiving letters in the mail from colleges and universities during my junior year of high school. In my household, the goal was to attend a school that provided a scholarship to keep expenses low.

As a result, I attended Lincoln University, the first HBCU, for my freshman year of college. However, after a year there, I became a bit more focused and knowledgeable about what I thought I wanted to major in and the type of experience I wanted from college. A few friends from high school told me about A&T and after researching the Journalism program, I made plans to transfer.

At the beginning of my sophomore year and from the very moment I stepped on campus; I knew I made the right decision. I joined the modeling troupe, Couture, the first year, and as part of Spirit Week, I proudly modeled Aggie paraphernalia on the runway with and for people that would remain a part of a history I didn't even know was forming at the time.

All I ever really knew about attending college was what I saw when watching *A Different World* on television as a kid. A&T's atmosphere, from the famous mural in the Student Union Building, to the lively conversations in the cafeteria to the Greek pride, was what I imagined and so much more.

One of my fondest memories at A&T was late nights at dance practice. I was a member (and eventually became the captain) of the Blue Reign dance team which performed in Corbett Gym during halftime at basketball games. I really enjoyed spending hours learning new choreography and coming up with creatively themed routines and costumes for our performances. When I first joined the dance team, I met the founder and captain, Monkeisha Borders. Keisha, to me, was a force to be reckoned with. She was bubbly and as sweet as Southern tea, but she also had high expectations. As the captain of the team, she led with fierce passion, enthusiasm, precision and purpose. She became a role model for me and would eventually become a Big Sister with whom I would forge a permanent bond.

My junior year, I became a Finer Woman of The Sophisticated Zeta Alpha Chapter of Zeta Phi Beta Sorority, Incorporated. As much as I would like to say I chose Zeta, I truly believe Zeta chose me. The motivation of its beloved Founders to form the organization to eradicate elitism in a time when division and classism between those who could attend college and those who were not so fortunate was honorable and admirable to me. Over 100 years later, I still observe this unfortunate division even among those who are college educated. As a young college student, it was important to me to be a part of an organization that prioritized the highest education standards and embraced differences among Black women. Becoming part of such an organization has not been met without its challenges, but unmatched sisterly bonds, a reputation for academic excellence and a rich, international legacy of trailblazers who always raise the bar and refuse to be molded into what society expects has been the reward. Being a Finer Woman was the only choice for me.

I went on to become a leader of the Zeta Alpha chapter, as Vice President, Step master and Dean of Pledges during my senior year. I learned so much about leadership, perseverance, and sisterhood from my experience on campus, and I became a role model for others. I also had a ton of fun participating in community service projects with my sorority sisters and fraternity brothers. *Sleep Out for the Homeless* was an event organized by my brothers of the Evil Eta Chapter of Phi Beta Sigma Fraternity, Incorporated where our organizations spend a Winter's night sleeping on the plot to raise funds and awareness for the homeless community. We would also serve meals and donate toys during the Christmas holiday. Greek life, in general, was unforgettable. The step shows were always a production during G.H.O.E. (Greatest Homecoming On Earth) and Aggie Fest. I remember long nights producing creative themes and concepts and practicing in empty parking lots and gyms for the big shows. The bright lights and loud chants and cheers as we performed for the audience of our peers was exhilarating and some of the most fun I've ever had.

As a broadcast journalism major, I had some amazing experiences. I was an intern at the Greensboro Newseum, where I was able to produce, direct and write a mini documentary about one of the Tuskegee Airmen. I was also an intern at WPGC 95.5FM, the number one hip-hop radio station in the DMV. My classes were always hands-on, and I gained so much practical experience both as a radio and television personality. I learned how to read from a teleprompter, record voice-overs, operate a camera, and produce my own commercials not just from a book or someone else's demonstration but through actual experience. My professors, especially Dr. Theresa

Styles and Ms. Gail Wiggins, will always be remembered for their love and passion for teaching and mentorship.

I decided to go to law school after working for three summers as a legislative assistant at a lobbying firm in DC. I was really inspired by the influence possessed by policymakers to make new laws and create social change, and it is something that continues to drive my enthusiasm, particularly as it relates to the precious and essential resource that is energy in this country. Once I made the decision to go to law school, I was able to take a prep course right on campus. A&T always had resources for my needs.

One of the best things about being an alumna of A&T is the pride and legacy that comes from the institution. I gained "framily" for life from A&T. No matter how long it's been, I know there are people I can call, and it will feel like we never lost touch. If I need something, they will provide it and they can expect the same from me. I know that if I show up to an event or even to the grocery store and Aggies are in the building, we will embrace like we've known one another all our lives. I've even met an Aggie on a submarine in the middle of the ocean in Maui! The camaraderie and zeal for the experiences we've all shared, the halls we've all walked, the songs and chants we remember, and the colors we proudly wear is a big part of it. But it's also about the confidence and knowledge we gained from an institution that taught us to be prideful in our blackness and our individualism. A&T has historically bred barrier breaking powerhouses like Janice Bryant Howroyd, the first African American woman to build and own a billion-dollar company, and Hilda Pinnix-Ragland, the first African American woman to serve as a vice president at Duke Energy, to name a few.

I carry the lessons I learned from A&T in all aspects of my life. I have continued to be a leader in philanthropy through nonprofit organizations like the Girl Scouts of Greater Chicago and Northwest Indiana and the Black Women Lawyers' Association of Greater Chicago. I am a thought leader in the energy industry on issues pertaining to supplier and workforce diversity and the importance of the integration of diverse perspectives in the clean energy transition in the United States.

Although I didn't ultimately become the next Ananda Lewis or the female Donnie Simpson, I gained a confidence in my voice that I owe completely to my time at the number one public HBCU in the nation. I have become the first Nakhia Crossley. She is resilient, resourceful, bold in her purpose, and unapologetically Black. She is a warrior.

About Nakhia Crossley

Nakhia Crossley is Central Region Director & Counsel at the Solar Energy Industries Association (SEIA), a national trade association dedicated to solar advancement, advocacy, and education. In her role, Nakhia oversees and implements regulatory and legislative strategy to advance the growing solar market in the region. With over a decade of legal experience, Nakhia previously worked for the Illinois Commerce Commission, in private practice at Schumacher Electric Corporation and as a law firm owner serving entrepreneurs. Throughout her career, Nakhia has been passionate about the advancement and empowerment of minorities, women and youth in both legal and S.T.E.M. careers. She currently serves as President of the Board of Directors at The Black Women Lawyers' Association of Greater Chicago, Inc., a Founding Associate Board Member of Girl Scouts of Greater Chicago/Northwest Indiana, and mentor and speaker for the Women's Energy Network and Women of Renewable Industries and Sustainable Energy (WRISE). Professionally, she has been featured in several publications for her energy regulatory expertise, including Public Utilities Fortnightly, Solar Power World, Crain's Chicago Business and the Chicago Daily Herald. She has been awarded for her leadership, diversity, and mentorship efforts, including as a Top 40 Under 40 Emerging Leader by Energy News Network, a Top 100 Under 50 Executive Leader by Diversity MBA Magazine, a Trailblazer and Emerging Leader in the law by the Black Women Lawyers' Association of Greater Chicago, Inc. and with the Honorable A. Leon Higginbotham Jr. Award by the National Bar Association. Nakhia earned her B.S. in Journalism/Mass Communications from North Carolina A&T State University and her J.D. from Thomas Jefferson School of Law in San Diego, CA. She is a 2020 Fellow of the Chicago Urban League and University of Chicago Booth School of Business IMPACT Executive Leadership Development Program.

KELVIN M. PRATT

When Did I Fall in Love with A&T
Kelvin M. Pratt

I loved A&T before I ever had my high school diploma. I'm from a small place called Anson County. Some people may have heard about it, but many people won't have a clue where it's located. We weren't privileged to do many things that other kids were able to experience. However, I just accepted the fact that I was raised a country boy. I appreciate and respect how I came up, but I always enjoyed city life. When I visited my extended family in Greensboro, I thought that I was in a big city. I loved to hear the stories about North Carolina A&T and the history of the famous Reverend Jesse Jackson and Dr. Ronald McNair, who attended the university. Even stories from the 1969 Uprising, the Greensboro Four, and other historical memories relative to North Carolina A&T.

Let's not forget the homecoming memories as a kid from the festivals and cookouts. It was love at first sight. When I was a young kid, I never felt like I met a stranger during the festivities. If you were hungry and thirsty, people looked out for you regardless. The history and foundation of North Carolina A&T alone helped me understand that I was making the right educational and moral decision for my college path.

As I reflect on my freshman year in college, I still can't believe it's already been 20 years. That year was very life-changing for me. I felt like I was growing up and beginning an unforgettable new chapter in my life. I convinced my right-hand partner, Shawnique, to come to A&T, be my roommate, and start his new chapter as an Aggie man also. We moved into Scott B; 3rd floor mid-August of 2001. Our parents were so excited to get us out of their houses and take our lives to another level. We met so many great people from all over the United States.

Some of the students were from small towns just like us, then other students from larger cities. I never realized I had a country accent until I went to college. People immediately said, "You're a country boy. I can tell by your accent." Everybody had their own style and represented culture to the best of their ability. I remember the first gym jam that we attended. A few of us guys from Scott B got fresh to go like we were Mike, Roland, and Slim from the movie, "The Wood." That was a memorable night, along with so many other days in the life of A&T.

There are times in life, you're going to experience tragedies no matter where you are located. Less than two months after being at A&T, I experienced two major tragedies in my life within a few days apart. On September 11, we experienced one of the worst terrorist attacks known to our generation. So many people lost family and friends due to one of the most pivotal points in American history. I remember just getting back to my room from a class and seeing it on the news about the first tower being hit. I was in complete shock. My friends from upstate were terrified of not reaching their families, and my heart went out to them. Like it happened yesterday, I recall whispering a prayer. At the same time, I felt the tears streaming down my face and asking God to watch over those people. Hearing the stories unfold was heartbreaking. As my roommate, Shawnique, and I continued watching the news, we couldn't believe what was happening before our eyes. About 10 minutes later, the phone rang, and it was my dad checking on us. I knew by my father being in law enforcement that the next few days would be busy. He told us to stay safe, and he'd come to check on us as soon as he could get away from work. He was able to visit the next day, and I was so happy to see my Pops. However, during this time, I didn't know that this week would be the last time seeing him alive. The last thing I remember my dad saying to me was, "Son, your mom and I are so damn proud of you. Remember why you came to college and don't get caught up with all these cute little girls. We love you, Marq, and tell Red (Shawnique) I will see him next time." A few days later, on September 14, 2001, I lost my father in a fatal car accident. He was headed to work that morning, and less than three miles away from the house I was raised in, an individual hit his law enforcement car, colliding head-on. That was absolutely the saddest day in my life.

Upon returning to classes after our tragic loss, my A&T community was there with nothing but support. Therefore, I fell in love with A&T even more. The empathy and love shown made it seem as if they lost a family member also. My professors called and checked on my family. They made sure I had the resources to catch back up when I returned to classes. On some days, I couldn't walk five minutes without getting a hug or friends checking on me. I remember when I saw Chancellor Renick in the student union. He stopped me and said, "Mr. Pratt, I'm sorry about your loss." My first thought was, how do you know exactly who I am but thank you, Chancellor Renick." From the greatest to the least, I was shown love which only deepened my love for North Carolina A&T.

The decision to attend North Carolina A&T was one of the best life decisions ever. It helped shape and mold me into the man that I am today. In addition, I've created some lifelong friendships! Some of those friends I speak to every day, some we see each other once or twice a year but pick up like we never left off, and some are gone but will forever be in my heart. Rest well, Bianca Richardson and Tacuma Cardwell.

To the Illustrious North Carolina Agricultural & Technical State University, I thank you for the life experience and the knowledge you bestowed upon me. You were a safe home away from home. Everything that you have taught me, I will instill into the younger generations. I will teach them the importance of HBCU's and the legacy that comes along with them.

To my Aggies Alum, I love you all! We will always be family, and GHOE will always be the annual family reunion! Aggie Born, Aggie Bred, I'm an Aggie till I'm Dead!

Love,
The Aggie That Doesn't Bother Nobody…

About Kelvin M. Pratt

Kelvin was raised in a small town within Anson County called Morven N.C. He fell in love with North Carolina A&T at an early age when attending events and visiting family in Greensboro. Kelvin later attended A&T for college and graduated with a Bachelor of Science in Political Science.

Kelvin currently lives in Charlotte N.C. where he is an Account Manager for ON24. During his leisure time he enjoys playing golf, road biking, and volunteering in the community. One of his goals is to bring more awareness and change to the kids of his hometown by implementing programs that focus on mental health, minority lifestyles, college & trade schools, entrepreneurship, and more.

The Best Decision I Ever Made
Veronica C. Hairston

As I close out every tour, I give at my alma mater North Carolina A & T State University, I end with the same phrase. "Going to North Carolina Agricultural and Technical State University was the best decision I've ever made!" I say this each time with the biggest smile on my face; however, the phrase is a serious matter to me. I want the student (potential future Aggies) and their families to understand that l am not trying to sell them a dream. Instead, I am trying to give them insight into my HBCU experiences.

I was not the best or the brightest student in high school; there was even a point where I thought I didn't want to go to college. That all changed the first time I stepped foot on the campus of Virginia State University. It was Homecoming 2002, and my cheerleading coach Shandra Claiborne wanted her squad to see her beloved alma mater. My love for HBCU came alive that day, although I already knew all about HBCU's. My father went to Virginia Union University in Richmond, Virginia. I also had two aunts on my father's side who were alumna at Spelman College and Livingstone College. My mother's older brother, who I never had the pleasure of meeting, was also an HBCU graduate. My mother would tell me stories all the time about his days at Howard University.

HBCUs were already in my blood, and now thanks to that trip to Virginia State, they were in my heart. Fast forward to Spring of 2004, and I'm doing the college tour rounds. I've visited Howard University and Hampton University on this tour, along with Old Dominion University. I told everyone I had no interest in going to a predominantly white institution. I had already been to countless college fairs and met so many HBCU alums that encouraged my decision. I worked concessions at MEAC tournaments, where I got my first glimpse of North Carolina Agricultural and Technical State University. However, my heart was still set on the Mecca at the time. Howard may have been the dream, but A&T, a public land grant institution, was much more affordable. I applied even though I never got a chance to tour the University, and when I was accepted, my heart told me that's where I was going to go. As much as I loved Virginia State and always wanted to cheer as a Woo Woo, it was far too close for me. Petersburg was just 30 minutes up the road from Richmond, Virginia. I was ready to spread my wings and fly out of Virginia!

I found myself on North Carolina A & T State University's campus, where my mother cried as she unpacked the last of my things, and I rejoiced at my first taste of adult freedom. But, getting to A&T was only the beginning of my journey. Now I needed to find out exactly who I was and what I was capable of. My HBCU is where I met lifelong friends who are more like extended family. My HBCU is where I sharpened my leadership skills in Student Government Association. My HBCU gave me mentors who still support me to this day. My HBCU allowed me to gain membership in the FIRST sorority for black college-trained women, Alpha Kappa Alpha Sorority Incorporated. The Alpha Phi chapter will forever be in my heart. I was able to give of myself through service to my community and fellow students. Later on, I was privileged to give to a whole new generation of Aggies, but I'll get to that later.

North Carolina A&T State University is a history-rich land grant institution with a strong focus on STEM that has grown so much since I was a freshman in the fall of 2005. Now in 2021, we are the largest HBCU in the country, with over 13,300 total students. Currently, I have the honor of serving as the Assistant Director of Student Activities and Campus Involvement. My office manages several of our Big Five organizations on campus. These same organizations were regularly a part of my college experience. As a member of the Student Government Association, we worked closely with the Student Union Advisory Board (SUAB). I have been able to watch SUAB's growth as an organization and restructuring. SUAB is now the Student University Activities Board, and they manage major campus programming throughout the institution. There is no longer a Mister Aggie or Miss SUAB. They have expanded their program chairs to have positions like Gaming and Cinema Chair, Concert and Lively Arts, and Diversity and Inclusions Chair. I remember participating in SUAB activities on campus as an undergrad. It is a treat to see how they have expanded to be involved in national organizations like the National Association of Campus Activities. They have aligned themselves with campus programming boards from across the country and/or the premiere programming group on campus.

My department also manages the Council of Presidents (COP). If you were a part of any on-campus organizations, you must have interacted with the Council of Presidents. They are the governing body of all campus organizations. Like SUAB, COP has been able to reinvent itself into an organization that truly advocates for the needs of the students they represent. The group now manages 1891 Connect, which is a way for all students to interact and engage with our campus organizations. The best way to figure out what exactly is happening on campus is to check 1891 Connect. I continue to be so impressed with the ways our students are helping to improve university processes. They assist our staff in researching and developing ways to make student engagement more accessible and convenient for the students they serve.

Service is a central theme of this chapter. One of the best ways we exhibit and highlight service on campus is through our Greek-letter organizations. As a proud product of a Greek- letter organization on campus, I know the Office of Fraternity and Sorority Engagement's value. You may remember that the office used to be called the Greek Life office for any alumni reading this. As the office has changed, the structure of how its organizations is governed has changed as well.

The office is no longer broken up into two organizations. Instead, I have created a joint Greek Council that governs all Greek organizations on campus for the National Pan Hellenic Council and other organizations that are not a part of the divine. As a result, the students continue to win awards, be nationally recognized, and represent the best of what North Carolina A&T is. Being a part of Greek-letter organizations is an exceptional experience. With distinction, our students continue to represent our national organizations and the chapters that we hold so near and dear to our hearts.

Of course, I have to discuss the organization that I supervise and hold close to my heart. Student Government Association is the advocating body for current students at North Carolina A&T State University. They are responsible for ensuring that students are heard and represented on campus. Student Government Association has a long history of advocacy and dedication to students. A&T alum like members of the A&T Four, Jesse Jackson, and even Terrence J. have allowed SGA to shape their leadership abilities. We have seen a shift in the goals of the organization in recent years. Students have focused less on programming and more on advocating. They are making sure they find space at the table for students to be heard. A push for seeing students on all standing university committees was made in the late 2010's. We see more students actively serve their fellow students and uphold their advocacy, leadership, and engagement each year.

I know many of these chapters will reflect on past memories from our undergraduate and possibly master's experiences at North Carolina A&T State University. I am so blessed to have been able to get two degrees from this institution. I was hired to come back and work for my alma mater. My reflection touches on how I got here and what I have experienced as I have grown. In my professional career at A&T, I have witnessed the transformation of many organizations that touch our students.

Moreover, I have seen these programs and organizations be a service to me. I have reciprocated those experiences to be of service to others, and now I serve the next generation of Aggie student leaders. Each time I'm able to reflect on my experiences and development through A&T, I can confidently say that coming to North Carolina A&T State University was the best decision I ever made!

About Veronica Camille Hairston

Veronica Camille Hairston was born and raised in Richmond, Virginia. She earned both her bachelor's degree in Family Consumer Sciences and master's degree in Adult Education with a concentration in Higher Education Administration from North Carolina A&T State University. Currently, she serves as Assistant Director in the Office of Student Activities and Campus Involvement at North Carolina A&T. She has a background in programming and event development in both the non-profit and educational sectors.

Before returning to her alma mater, Veronica held positions in the Guilford County School System and International Civil Right Center and Museum. Veronica is a product of Student Government Association at NC A&T under the Bass Administration (2008-2009) and now has the honor of serving as advisor for the organization.

She was honored as the 2020 Advisor of the Year Award by the HBCU Kings and Queens Conference. In 2021 she was recognized as the Xceleader Advisor of the Year. Both awards required student nomination which made the recognition even more meaningful. She is a student-centered professional who focuses on the growth and development of the student leaders she manages.

Veronica is a Spring 2007 initiate of the Alpha Phi chapter of Alpha Kappa Alpha Sorority, Incorporated and currently maintains active membership in the Beta Iota Omega Chapter in Greensboro, NC. She is married to Gregory Carl Hairston, Jr., who serves as the Senior Associate Athletics Director for External Affairs at NC A&T, and they have a Pomeranian named Hershey.

ANSEN JONES

Photo Credit: Kiirstn Pagan

Take 2
Ansen Jones

My HBCU experience was phenomenal. There were bad times and there were good times. The bad times helped shape the good, and the good times made it great. My experience started at Florida A&M University (FAMU); however, by the end of my freshman year, I decided to transfer closer to home. In reality, I wanted to transfer to be closer to my high school sweetheart who went to Hampton University. I decided to transfer to North Carolina A&T State University (NCA&T). Aside from FAMU being an awesome school, and being known as a great business school, I was lucky enough to get in-state tuition at FAMU. This decision was probably the best decision I have made my entire adult life, and it played a major role in my development.

Unlike most of my friends who were inspired to go to HBCUs because they have family history within, my desire to go to an HBCU started in high school. I graduated in 2000 from Long Reach High School in Columbia, Maryland. At the time, Columbia was considered the melting pot of Maryland for its diversity in ethnicity, religion, and economical class. This stimulated the desire for myself and a lot of my classmates to apply to HBCUs. My classmates had legitimate reasons to apply and go to Clark, FAMU, Hampton, Howard, NCA&T, Spelman, and Tuskegee, to name a few. I initially chose FAMU because, on my HBCU tour, as we drove through Tallahassee, all I remember was seeing southern girls promoting a car wash. It was in that moment that I made the decision to major in business!

FAMU was the foundation and ice breaker of my HBCU experience. I graduated from high school and headed to the "hill".

Seeing the magnitude of the environmental "code switching" going up the "hill," noticing a legit difference across the train tracks between FSU and FAMU, felt like home. Attending FAMU was a cultural shock for me. Growing up as an Air Force brat, then becoming a Jessup/Columbia, Maryland implant surrounded by diversity, it was a shock. But I was amazed and excited to experience so many motivated and determined people like me. The magnitude of diversity within the black culture was *eye opening*. It was exhilarating to see and, ultimately, it was the beginning of an amazing experience.

When I arrived, I was not alone. There were quite a few people from back home. That was a relief that I had people I could lean on. I ended up living in campus apartments, not dorms, I cancelled my meal plan, MISTAKE, but one night I had no food in my apartment and both of my roommates where gone. I called a classmate from Long Reach… I said, "yo bro, you hungry? What you got to eat?" He said, "yeah man, but we don't have $h*T here but a jar of spaghetti sauce," I laughed and said "bet, I don't have anything but spaghetti noodles, I am on the way!" The unconditional connection with folks from home was great. But the HBCU experience introduces you to black people from all walks of life. The barbers, the beauticians, the athletes, the rappers and musicians, the "hustle men" (natural born entrepreneurs) were all there. Two of the first people I met and instantly bonded with were from different walks of life. He was from Nashville, the dorm barber, and a master chest player, while she was from Milwaukee, a ball player, and a mathematician (at least to me). Two of the best people I met at FAMU.

When I first arrived at FAMU, I fell in love with *all* that I saw. I just knew I wanted to be there; however, it was not where I was meant to be. I did have a blast while I was there. Met some awesome people, participated in as many extracurricular activities as my schedule would allow, and most importantly, my classes were centrally located to my dorm room at Sampson Hall. So making 8am classes was a breeze, rolling out of bed at 0730, brushing my teeth, and strolling to class with sweats and flip flops on was too easy. But, as much as I enjoyed FAMU, something was missing. I felt like I was not living up to the standard. I was living in the shadows of my twin brother's success (who is now a USAF Academy graduate, a Lieutenant Colonel fighter pilot and commander). His success was definite, all while I was still searching for who I was. So, I thought about the military. Then, I simply decided to transfer.

There I was, a second-semester freshman at a new school. I'd already broken into the joys of being at an HBCU. But surprisingly, I still felt lost knowing no one or who even from home was there. Subsequently, neither my transfer to North Carolina A&T, nor my transition, went smoothly. But there was no one to blame except myself. Then, September 11th happened. Shortly after arriving at school and checking into Cooper Hall, I ended up leaving and joining the U.S. Army Reserves for many reasons. But the extra money for school was a plus. My training took me through the 2001 school year, so I did not return until the fall of 2002.

I was homeless. Broke. Lonely. Afraid. These trying times contributed to my awesome experience. I was determined to fulfill someone's prophecy about me. I just couldn't afford tuition and room and board. My parents worked hard, but they did not exactly contribute to the bills of my higher education. I had my father's 1996 Dodge Conversion van that he didn't know I lived out of and a little bit of money my mother gave me monthly. Unbeknownst to her, I used to keep the lights on (gas in the van) and I had my drill pay.

In the fall of 2002, I returned to school, and, through my reserve unit, I met a few Aggies. In between sleeping in the van, I spent nights on cots, couches and dorm floors. The comradery was real … unbreakable! That semester, I also enrolled in the ROTC program and remember writing that one of my goals was to earn a combat patch. In January of 2003, I was withdrawn from school in support of Operation Iraqi Freedom.

The majority of my unit was split between young students and disgruntled old farts who had deployed in Desert Storm. None of them really cared for our enthusiasm or erratic behavior. Surprisingly, most of us students were Aggies with a sprinkle of Bennett Belles. Our unit was paired up with a unit consisting of South Carolina State Bulldogs! Oh, the arguments we had, the laughs we shared, and the tears we shed representing our HBCUs deployed. We were like siblings. We talked about each other's universities regularly but dared someone outside the "family" to do so, and the bond was natural. This deployment contributed a lot to my personal growth, but it also enhanced my love and respect for HBCUs.

I returned from Iraq in the spring of 2003, unemployed, with my oldest son two months from being born, all the while waiting for school to start. By the fall of 2004, as a second-semester sophomore, I was a full-time student, employee and father. In 2005, I became a member of the Beta Epsilon chapter of Alpha Phi Alpha Fraternity, Inc. While I regret not being financially active, joining Beta Epsilon was life-altering and a better experience than I expected seeking fellowship and brotherhood, following in my father's footsteps. I experienced a ton of growth. I got comfortable being uncomfortable, and I learned from people I otherwise probably would have never met as a nontraditional student. Being a nontraditional student was difficult, but I think it kept me grounded. It kept me grounded because I couldn't just up and go as I wanted to. I couldn't hang out all the time, party hard, and stay up late. It added that balance that I needed for personal growth. Subsequently, I think people respected me more because I had some structure and displayed a sense of responsibility.

I made my experience good. Life, through people and circumstances, made my experience great. But North Carolina A&T made life awesome.

I love my circle, and I love my HBCUs… AGGIE PRIDE! - RIH J. Matt - 9SLFM4L

About Ansen Jones

Ansen Jones is currently a Project Manager working towards Program Management with several years of experience with operational execution and andragogy in professional, tactical, and austere environments. Ansen is very passionate about creating an enjoyable work environment while simultaneously mentoring junior level employees on the benefits of exposing their potential for personal and professional growth. He is infamous for randomly telling "dad jokes" for personal gratification and is known for saying, "I tell jokes to make me laugh, if you laugh, that's just a bonus."

He is an Air Force brat, but spent the majority of his childhood in Jessup, Maryland and graduating from Long Reach High School in Columbia, MD. He has a Bachelor of Arts degree in Professional English from North Carolina A&T State University and a Masters of Business Administration, with a concentration in Project Management, from Liberty University. His affiliated organizations include Prince Hall Mason, Alpha Phi Alpha Fraternity Incorporated, and he has proudly served our country. He is a veteran of the United States Army and has multiple deployments in support of several campaigns, in Southwest Asia, as a soldier and a civilian. Ansen takes pride in his job and all that he has accomplished. As a result, he feels fortunate to be afforded the ability to continuously support the troops home and abroad.

While primarily operating in the capacity of project manager, Ansen is a Senior Operations and Training Analyst for an engineering firm in the Baltimore Metropolitan area. With over 12 years of experience in management, training, and operations, he provides subject matter expertise, and management services in an International Programs division within the Department of Defense. Most importantly, Ansen loves spending time with his kids; taking them bowling, to Baltimore Orioles games, and amusement parks. He is modern-day Renaissance man, professional, leader, and father!

PATRICE MURPHY

From Legacy to Leader
Patrice Murphy

When thinking of Patrice Murphy, one may think of the phrase, "Aggie Born and Aggie Bred" because I come from a long line of Aggies: my parents, uncles, aunts, brother, and a host of cousins. The family legacy began with two freshmen at North Carolina A&T State University. In 1971, my parents met; they gradually went from study partners to life partners. A few years after graduation, in 1975, they got married and started a family in Clinton, MD. We were an inseparable family of five: my parents; my brother, Jay (the oldest); my sister, Toya (the middle); and, of course, myself (the youngest, also known as "the baby"). There was one phrase that we would constantly hear when growing up in my childhood home: "Murphy Pride!" It wasn't just our family mantra; it was a value system instilled in us from birth. Taking pride in everything we did and knowing who we represented while doing it. This mantra created a strong work ethic, a passion for helping people, and natural leadership.

As the youngest of three, I naturally followed the legacy of my brother and sister throughout life. From the three of us attending the same schools to my sister and I participating in all the same activities. In short, if one did it, we all did it. When it came to college however, we had a choice... well, kind of. There was only one HBCU, and that was A&T. I inquired about others, but it was clear I was going to A&T, and I appreciate my parents' strong encouragement because it was the best decision we could've made. While I admired and appreciated the great examples of those that came before me, I made it my mission to stand out and create my own lane in everything in which I participated. My tenure at North Carolina A&T State University was no different.

As a trained dancer, I wanted to continue dancing while at A&T, but I wasn't sure of the best route. My brother, fellow Aggie alum, said, without hesitation, "you have to join Golden Delight, they are a part of the band, but that's the best dance team on campus." Following his advice, I auditioned for Golden Delight in the summer of 2003; little did I know my college career would begin immediately. I was so excited and eager to dance, but I never took a moment to educate myself on what I had gotten myself into by joining the Blue & Gold Marching Machine. The amount of pride, and sheer passion for their talents and gifts that was demonstrated by my teammates and band members, was unmatched. There were several days that I questioned myself and wanted to give up, but there was that family mantra that helped me push through, "Murphy Pride." Although I got a crash course on what being in the band, in the south, is like, I wouldn't trade it for anything. Discipline, teamwork, and sacrifice are priceless life skills I learned in the band, but what is equally as rewarding is that I was the first in my family to perform in the university band.

In the Spring of 2005, I embarked on a journey that would be another family first: I was initiated into the Alpha Mu chapter of Delta Sigma Theta. I immediately took the bull by the horns and stepped up to the plate to best represent my chapter. From Miss Alpha Mu to Step Master, and First Vice President it was extremely important for me to not only best represent the chapter, but also represent for myself and my family, "Murphy Pride." Leadership is not an easy feat and leading my peers challenged me in an entirely different way. The key to my success was humility and transparency; they played a huge role in how I approached my positions, understanding the importance of being true to myself first then others around me. While the step master, we raised $10,000 for the chapter in one year, which had never been done before. That is a true testament to teamwork amongst the ladies in the chapter.

Upon graduating, with a Biology Pre-Med Degree, in 2007, I began shadowing local physicians while working in pharmaceutical sales. Although sales made me a solid income, I knew that I was not "helping people" like I set out to. Some of the medications I was encouraging doctors to prescribe to their patients did more harm than good. In November of 2015, I decided it was time to use my gifts and help people in my own way. I birthed my own fitness company: Curves and Gains Fitness. My mission was to help men, women, and youth live happier and healthier lives through exercise and balanced nutrition.

A few short months later, in April of 2016, I was laid off from pharmaceutical sales. I knew that was my nudge from God to take a leap of faith into full entrepreneurship. Out of everything I had overcome and accomplished in life, this, by far, was the scariest and proudest moment. I did not let fear stand in my way, I decided to hit the ground running with nothing but a few clients and my faith in God.

Naturally, I was faced with challenges through the years, but the work ethic it required to graduate with a biology degree while participating in campus activities helped me push through. Remembering all the long nights studying in the library before organic chemistry exams prepared me for the long hours I'd have to put in as a CEO and personal trainer. Even remembering the days, I had band practice before and after class prepared me for having clients all day from 5 am to 8 pm.

By 2017, my company had significantly grown, and I was blessed to employ three of my friends. I learned that being a business owner isn't all about what you can do for yourself, but it's how, and who, you impact in the process. In 2018 Washington, DC's own Radio One recognized me as a "Millennial Making Moves" for leaving corporate America and running a successful fitness company.

We all know what 2020 brought, an immeasurable amount of change. Change in the way we approached business, school, and work. One thing that remained constant amongst so much change was my passion and will to help people become the best version of themselves. In May of 2020, we closed the doors of the gym, a place I had called home for nearly five years. I knew I needed to reshape, refocus, and reimagine what it meant to be a CEO and Personal Trainer. But, more importantly, how to serve a community of people who needed me more than ever.

In addition to the physical training, I developed and coached my clients on the concept of "You vs You." Understanding you have the power to make long lasting lifestyle changes to help you reach your goals. Equally you are the sole person who can get in the way of achieving your goals. This mindset coaching is what separates Curves and Gains Fitness from your ordinary fitness company. The physical change will not happen without the mental and emotional shift. That is how I have been able to change the lives of countless people for almost six years. I have helped people reverse diabetes, lose weight postpartum, lower their blood pressure, fit into wedding dresses, amongst many other life-changing milestones.

These are not skills you learn in business school; they are the life lessons I learned as an Aggie Legacy. I learned that leaders face adversity head-on, and they do not let fear of change get in the way of serving. They say that the true test of leadership is how you function in a crisis. Well, in 2021, I rose to the occasion and developed an online platform to reach a much larger audience beyond the DC, Maryland, and Virginia areas. My clientele now ranges from New York to California and everything in between. I have landed contracts with United Health Care, District of Columbia Government Agencies, Uncensored TV Network and the City of District Heights Mayor.

My journey through entrepreneurship has been far from easy. I questioned myself and wanted to quit many times. There was no roadmap from Aggie legacy to the first, full-time entrepreneur in the family. Different from my childhood where I always had someone to whom I could ask, "What do I do next?" I had to rely on my faith in God, my education, and my passion to help people guide me through. Now when I'm asked to whom I attribute my success, my response is my core values: perseverance, leadership, and "Murphy Pride". I evolved from Legacy to Leader.

About Patrice Murphy

Patrice Murphy graduated from North Carolina A&T State University in the 2007 with a Bachelor of Science in Biology. Following the legacy of her parents James and Mareitta Murphy, Class of '75 and a host of family she is the epitome of "Aggie Born & Aggie Bred". While attending North Carolina A&T State University, Patrice diversified her experience by joining both social and educational organizations. In 2003 she performed in The Blue & Gold Marching Machine as a Golden Delight, affectionately known as the "Sweethearts of the MEAC". In 2005 she was initiated into the Alpha Mu Chapter of Delta Sigma Theta Sorority, Incorporated and joined the Biology Club.

Patrice Murphy has led an impressive career as a CEO and personal trainer in her six years working in the Fitness industry. In 2018, she was named "Millennial Making Moves" by Washington DC's own Radio One for leaving the corporate world and starting her own professional and personal training company, Curves and Gains Fitness. Patrice has also been featured in several well-known publications, including the City of District Heights Mayor's Office, United Health Care Wellness Division, DC Government Health & Wellness Division, and The Uncensored TV Network.

Serving as a personal trainer and online fitness coach at Curves and Gains Fitness. Patrice plays a major role in helping people achieve their health and fitness goals while learning a healthy balance of diet and exercise without having to compromise living life to the fullest. Through her commitment to this role, she has changed the lives of countless people by teaching them key healthy lifestyle skills to sustain long term results.

Prior to the birth of Curves and Gains Fitness, Patrice worked as a Pharmaceutical Sales Representative. During that role, she cultivated profitable relationships with physicians to close the deal using her unprecedented negotiation skills. Within her career as a Pharmaceutical Sales Representative, she worked in several specialties to include Pulmonology, Cardiology and Dermatology from 2007 to 2016.

Patrice originates from Clinton, MD in Prince George's County. When she is not working diligently to grow her fitness company she is volunteering in the community or at church. Spending time with her entire family however is her favorite past time. As an Auntie of six and parents within four miles of her home she never forgets the family mantra "Murphy Pride".

TRACY ALEXANDER

Exactly Where God Wanted Me to Be

Tracy Alexander

The "757," as we call it, is where I will forever call home. It's more widely known as Hampton Roads or Tidewater, and I grew up specifically in Chesapeake. I was raised by an amazingly smart and hardworking mother, a step-father who sacrificed for us and raised my brother and me as no less than his own, and my older brother, who was a much easier child for my parents to raise than I. My extended family rounded out my tribe and the backbone of my existence: grandparents, an aunt, an uncle, and cousins. My first cousin and I were only twelve days apart in age, and the four of us grandkids grew up like siblings. The neighborhood in which I grew up was a safe haven for me. I was always an extrovert, and that includes in the classroom. Though some would say I was talkative in school, I liked to think of myself as outspoken; however, getting good grades always came easy for me. Chesapeake was a place where the schools were of good quality and the neighborhoods were filled with hardworking people who were engaged in their kids' lives. I always had a close-knit group of friends who were more like family. It was this upbringing that prepared me to confidently leave home and go to North Carolina Agricultural and Technical State University, or North Carolina A&T for short.

I struggle to even remember why I ended up going to North Carolina A&T, and that, in and of itself, is the reason I know it was exactly where God wanted me to be. I legitimately can't recall when or how I even learned about A&T, but my first memories of it are from my Junior year in high school when my friends started taking college tours. I was the drum major of the band and couldn't miss the Friday games, so that meant missing out on touring the various colleges in the region. My friends came back from those tours enthusiastic about what they had seen–so much so, I could FEEL their passion for it. And even though I had never stepped foot on A&T's campus, I somehow knew it was the place for me. During my senior year of high school, I found myself considering Howard University because my cousin, who is more like a sister, was going there; we had never gone to different schools. However, my destiny as an Aggie became solidified once I met a young lady majoring in Chemical Engineering during a summer internship at NASA Langley Research Center. A&T came there for a career fair and not only had that very program but also scholarship opportunities; it was fate and my destiny into Aggie Land was sealed that summer of 2000.

I had the privilege of being invited to join the SMET (Science Math Engineering and Technology) program during the Summer of 2001 before my freshman year began. It was during that program that I was not only able to learn the campus and get used to college-paced courses, but I met amazing people who would become my lifelong friends. Relationships and bonds were formed that summer that forever changed me, and I will always be grateful for that. That experience set the foundation for me to go into my freshman year confidently; I had friends I could rely on, I knew how to get around campus, and some of the professors had already become familiar faces.

Walking the halls of McNair is indescribable; the College of Engineering is chock-full of Black excellence. I was blessed to matriculate amongst the most diverse group of young Black scholars I had ever seen. I'm almost ashamed to admit it was there that I learned just how diverse Black people, and our experiences, are. My life experiences had largely shown me only a microcosm of Black people, but, at A&T, I realized just how amazingly unique and eclectic we are. The Honors Program built, for me, a great foundation; Dr. Sandrea Williamson played an integral part in that program and ensured that I felt seen and cared for. I could always go to her office to talk through anything I needed, and she would always encourage me whenever I was struggling with something.

Courses as a ChemE major were challenging, but I'm grateful for my tribe. I was able to study and learn with some of the brightest young minds I had ever known. My friends were all majoring in challenging programs, so there was always a high level of accountability amongst the group. We all knew why we were there and what we came to accomplish; I never felt any pressure to do things that didn't serve my overall purpose in life. However, so much fun was still had! The first few years in Aggie Suites, playing games in the lobbies and hanging in each other's rooms, the epic house parties my roommates threw in Collegiate Commons in our latter years are all memories that I will cherish forever. I still remember the countless lunch meetups over the Chick-fil-A that didn't quite taste like Chick-fil-A and I can't begin to quantify how many Pizza Hut personal pan pizzas or Krispy Kreme donuts I consumed. This was, of course, in the days after the cafeteria was no longer in a trailer – only Aggies of a certain age will remember that! I certainly had more than my share of fun and memories to last a lifetime.

I had a variety of experiences throughout my four years that I truly enjoyed: being in the VA Aggies Club as a freshman and playing in the concert band my first two years (I was constantly in awe of the sheer talent of all the musicians) are two of the most notable. My fellow ChemE friends and I were active members in the American Institute of Chemical Engineers (AIChE) and traveled, annually, to their convention; we were always one of only a few HBCU chapters in attendance, and I never took for granted being a part of the representation that was missing. I was very fortunate to find a church home I loved, and I became very involved in the young adult ministry, including the weekly Bible studies. It was at this church that I joined the young adult dance team and had one of the most defining experiences of my college days. To be able to minister through dance was such a joy for me and something I have carried with me into adulthood.

Going to the university that produces the most, black engineers in the country comes with so many privileges, including access to companies for jobs and internships. I was blessed to land an internship after my sophomore year and each summer thereafter. These internships helped lead me to the career I've had for the last fifteen years: a Process/Process Safety Engineer. Being on the other side, as a recruiter at A&T for my company, I always take great pride in my efforts to bring more Aggies into my company knowing just how amazingly talented and capable they are.

My growth and maturity into adulthood began on the NC A&T campus. It is where I learned to work in teams, resolve conflict, be responsible for my own bills, and how to appropriately manage my time. A&T is where I gained the confidence in my knowledge and abilities to be able to go into a world that often doubts me, as a Black woman, knowing what I bring to the table. It is where I was able to fully step into, and cultivate, the God-given talents I had been born with. It's where I learned to be unapologetically me. I didn't even realize at the time this grooming was happening. It wasn't until I started my career, and had moments where I faced adversity, where I realized I was leaning heavily on this confidence that had been homegrown and instilled in me in Aggie Land to help me overcome challenges. Aggie Pride, for me, runs deep.

About Tracy Alexander

Tracy Alexander was born and raised in Chesapeake, VA. After graduating high school, she ventured off to North Carolina Agricultural and Technical State University where she graduated magnum cum laud in 2005 with a B.S. in Chemical Engineering. During her matriculation at NC A&T, Tracy was blessed to meet many of her lifelong friends while also interning at various Chemical and Oil and Gas companies. This experience led her to Shell Oil Company where she has worked the last 15 years as an engineer in Texas, Louisiana and Pennsylvania which she currently calls home. She specializes in Process Safety/Technical Safety Management and has huge passion for the health and safety of her colleagues and the community in which she works.

Outside of her job as an engineer, Tracy started Alex Lynn Virtual Assistance when she recognized most of her friends were entrepreneurs who had a wide variety of needs for the daily management of their personal businesses and lives. Task that most struggle to find the time to do or things that don't add the most value to their business, Tracy has a natural talent for and takes pleasure in doing. It is her goal to work closely with Black female Entrepreneurs / Small Business Owners to help them manage work-life balance and get the most value out of their time.

Tracy has a great passion for travel and has been blessed to see the world with Australia and New Zealand being among her favorite destinations so far. When she's not working, she enjoys learning and practicing her new fitness obsession, Olympic Weight Lifting. She is a "dog mom" to a spoiled yorkie named Zoe Isabel.

CHANCE D. LYNCH, ESQ.

North Carolina A&T: *To Be Young, Gifted and Black*
Chance D. Lynch, Esq.

Mumbling, chatter, daps and convos of upperclassmen reminding the newest Aggie class to be in Harrison Auditorium at 7pm... this was one of the first memories I have as a freshman at NC A&T. I did not understand why it was so important that I get to Harrison, but the crowd was going, so why not? I walked in, curious, bopping to the sounds of 102.5 and struggling to focus because Aggies were dancing, chanting, stepping and representing. I was submerged into a splendid cultural awareness of an inherited potential, I had yet to realize. The environment was more than entertaining - it was embracive and provoking. I was being challenged in a new way. Coming from eastern North Carolina, where natives were still dependent on outhouses, I was finally provoked to focus on the potential within me more than the proclivities in front of me.

I had found my tribe. My people. A home. I found a place that believed in me before I arrived. I was confident that I'd have the same confidence in what I would contribute to this culture that this culture would contribute to me. I wasn't home sick because I was away from home; I was sick because I was just finding it. The theme became so apparent and its applicability to my life became literally tangible. So tangible that it somehow became more than black words on white paper and much greater than a night of singing and entertainment - the theme was me and I was it - to be *"young, gifted and black."*

This was momentous. I was finally at a Historically Black College and University. Listen, this was a big deal. I had beaten the odds of failure predicted by those in my hometown. I had survived the odds of being the common statistic that was unfairly projected, not because of wasted talent but lack of interest from outsiders to discover it. This was huge. This was historical, indeed.

Historical - not because of its longevity, but it's resounding endurance. I was a resident on a university campus that not only survived Jim Crow but pioneered a movement against it. Historical, not because of its ancient infrastructure but its impact on the world. My school impacts every sector of the world as we know it. From the economist and accountants produced in Craig Hall to the historians trained in the classrooms of Warmoth T. Gibbs. From the undiscovered talent emerging from Alex Haley or the leading black engineers rising from Ronald McNair Hall. I realized in that sacred moment of self-realization and epiphany; I was no longer a student of history - I was part of it. The history I had read and studied had now become my reality and it was shaping me each day, in unimaginable ways, to be the person I am now. While some processes in the black college experience were found frustrating and a trial of patience, it taught me that life is not always fast and fair. Sometimes you have to plant your feet, take a brace, see it through, all while keeping your head held high.

"To be young..."

NC A&T taught me from the first day on campus that being young was not a disadvantage. It was an opportunity. I was inspired by my peers to embrace my youth and pursue everything ahead of me. I sat in that auditorium, silently anxious but thriving with motivation. I discovered a drive within me that I did not know existed. I was in shock. I had only been an Aggie for maybe a week and my perspective on life was rapidly changing. I was being challenged in a new way. It wasn't my first time away from home so I easily adjusted to the independence. Sure, I was "broke" and having just enough money to grab a Ms. Winner's dinner was a win. But none of that is uncommon to undergraduate students. Navigating the campus, juggling the social life and the vigorous demands of academia were certainly a challenge, but that night in Harrison awakened a pursuit in me that was ignited and remains ablaze. It made me young and fearless. I believe that is one commonality alumni from HBCUs share. There isn't much that scares us and if it is intimidating, we are taught from day one to do it while afraid. At times, age and youth share a negative connotation, and though a level of naivety is surely there, it won't limit one who is teachable. I sat there among some of the most brilliant, young minds in the world and we became students of North Carolina A&T. We became her proteges and accomplices in sustaining and continuing to mark the world with her rich history and contributions. Yes, I was young, but I was ambitious and this continues to ring true today. I gained so much from that moment. While others reminisced on the infamous "freshman 15", I can only remember the fire and fortitude that began to develop in me from the moment I became an Aggie.

"gifted..."

The room was filled with more than big city dialect and southern accents; I was sitting among the nation's rising politicians, educators, "movers and shakers." I began to internally search for the hidden gifts within myself. I learned at that moment that the world is filled with equal talent, but rarely provides equal opportunity. The speakers, poets and orators in Harrison that night challenged me in their own way, to create my own paths if they were never afforded to me. One of the greatest memories I have while at A&T was serving in the student senate and student government. I gained an appreciation for policy, making financial stewardship, and decision making. Our legislative body made huge strides that forged our school forward. For example, our senate voted, established and approved the position, "Mr. North Carolina A&T State University." We did not know that this role would play such a huge part in representing our culture to the world, but it has. Whether it was a fashion show by Verge, one of our modeling troupes, an incredible performance by Couture, oratory by our campus leaders, the sounds of cymbals and cleats echoing from the pavement from our marching band – every Aggie had a gift that contributed to the legacy of A&T. I was not a novice to public speaking when I arrived at A&T. I was a licensed minister and had served in leadership as youth for several years before college, but A&T gave me the tools and compass I needed to develop a life and career to giving voice to the indigent, standing shoulder-to-shoulder with the oppressed and serving the underserved. Whether in the pulpit or the courtroom, my life committed to serving others was solidified in college. One of my favorite academicians and fellow fraternity brother of Omega Psi Phi Fraternity, Incorporated, Dr. Benjamin Elijah Mays said, "We make our living by what we get; we make our lives by what we give." My alma mater taught me just that. I have learned that a living without a life has little value. What we give means more than anything we will ever get.

"...and black."

In a society where black is often viewed as a deficiency, NCA&T taught me that it was a commodity. I left Harrison that night with a fire to carry the rich tradition of NC A&T into every platform and corporate meeting room, in every philanthropic effort and all of life's goals and ambitions. It was a fire that prejudice couldn't weaken, and obstacles couldn't not extinguish. I learned who I am and how unstoppable I really was because of that knowledge. A native of Halifax County, North Carolina, I grew up in one of the poorest counties in North Carolina. But not only is poverty great, so is prejudice. Would you believe then and now, we have three school systems in one county? Should you survey the citizenry you may have mixed explanations, but the demographics shows a clear divide as a result of races. We have reached some milestones but the plight of being black in America is real and still relevant. Much has changed and much has remained the same. North Carolina A&T equipped me to pursue a law degree and I received a juris doctor from another prestigious HBCU, North Carolina Central University. The fire to fight for people who looked like me and those who were oppressed because of their race, gender, preference, socioeconomic status, and instability was fueled even more. I gained an appreciation for my color and struggles at these schools which made me a candidate to bring an end to these same struggles for others. These institutions taught me more than the uses of linguistics and phonetics, the mysteries of science and the formulas to mathematical equations. They taught me the importance of appreciating who you are and who God created you to be, before society tried to label you as who they perceived you to be. This is why our black colleges and universities are necessary.

My historically black school didn't teach me how to operate in society. It taught me how to be *black* and operate in it. Like roses that bloom in concrete spaces, Aggies are resolute and resilient. We are bold and fierce. We lead and create spaces for those around us to thrive. We are filled with pride because of this. We create. We reform. Aggies do.

About Chance D. Lynch, Esq.

Chance D. Lynch is a native of Enfield, Halifax County, North Carolina. He earned an English degree from North Carolina A&T State University, Greensboro, NC in 2006 and a Juris Doctor from North Carolina Central University School of Law, Durham, NC in 2009. He began his legal career as an Assistant District Attorney in Halifax County and then as a criminal defense attorney. Over the last 12 years, Chance has served eastern North Carolina as one of its most sought-after attorneys. In 2020, Chance founded the legal practice in his home county, Lynch Law, PLLC., aiming to give voice to the oppressed and providing advocacy that strengthens. His unwavering commitment to serving the indigent and underserved has landed him on national matters, serving as legal counsel on several high-profile civil rights cases across the nation.

Chance's community activism is extensive. He leads and serves on community boards that span from North Carolina to New York City, NY. He is a lifetime member of Alpha Phi Omega National Coeducational Fraternity, Inc. and a member of Omega Psi Phi Fraternity, Inc. He is the author of *"Faith Made Me Do It: A 21 Day Devotional"* that was released in 2018. Chance and his wife, fellow Aggie, Christina, have been married for 7 years and have two amazing daughters, Zoey Noelle and Zion Jael. They both serve as the Senior Pastors of Faith Church, Greenville, NC.

CHEYLAINA FULTZ

HBCU Doubters: Oh, The Places You'll Go with an A&T Degree

Cheylaina Fultz

I remember being twelve years old when my Uncle Josh asked me which college I wanted to attend. I blurted out, "A&T!" I have no clue why I said A&T; I had never been to the campus, and I didn't know much about the school itself. I had a couple of cousins who went in the '90s, and an uncle who'd gone during the '60s, so maybe it had something to do with that. However, Uncle Josh quickly busted my bubble: he questioned why I would want to go to A&T instead of a Duke or Princeton; bless his heart and rest his soul. I'm sure he didn't mean any harm, but many (not all) African-Americans were of a similar mindset to my uncle: they believed HBCUs weren't the standard for "the real world," and that you wouldn't be able to find a job upon graduating from an HBCU.

The irony of it all is that his mother, my grandmother, and his three siblings all attended, and graduated from HBCUs. However, to my uncle's defense, he was in his prime during the civil rights movement and Jim Crow era. Due to the discrimination that he faced, I am positive that the statement he uttered about my school of choice, was an unfortunate reality for his generation. I can imagine many qualified, and overqualified, HBCU applicants being passed over for their underqualified white counterparts.

Oh, but if Uncle Josh was alive today, he would see just how wrong he was… just how wrong the world was. Knowing my uncle, I doubt he'd admit it, but he would certainly see how great I turned out due to my North Carolina A&T college experience and degree. He would see just how far an HBCU degree CAN take you.

Unfortunately, he didn't live long enough to see an African-American as the President of our country, let alone a black female,

HBCU graduate, as Vice-President of our country. Oh, but if Uncle Josh was alive today, he would see Kamala Harris, Joyce Beatty, Alma Adams, Stacey Abrams, Keisha Lance Bottoms, and plenty more HBCU women who proved to the world just how powerful a degree from an HBCU is!

My uncle died when I was fifteen years old. He didn't get to see me graduate from high school and go off to college, which meant he didn't get to see that I defied his judgment and became an Aggie anyway!

Now, would you believe me if I told you that I *only* applied to North Carolina Agricultural and Technical State University? Well, I did. There was one other HBCU in Washington, DC (that shall go unnamed in this HBCU edition) that I was interested in attending. When my mom told me that I had to stay in-state for college, I figured there was no point in wasting that college application money. Therefore, I went with the choice I made at twelve years old. I can't begin to stress to you just how pivotal my choice to attend North Carolina A&T would be to my future self.

The moment I stepped foot on campus as a seventeen-year-old during the 2005 Summer orientation, I knew I was in the right place. I could feel it. I instantly fell in love with the campus, the people, the city of Greensboro, but most of all the PRIDE. I was so ready to leave my small town; I'm sure I could have fallen in love with *any* place that had more than a few stoplights, but there was something that felt so right about being in Aggieland.

That summer, I made instant connections with the other freshman students, so, by the time the first semester started, I had some familiar faces with whom I could mingle. Once school officially started, I realized just how diverse we as a people are: black people cannot be put into a box. We come from different backgrounds, states, countries, and cultures. One of the best parts about attending North Carolina A&T is that I got to experience many of those cultures all in one place. I learned about mambo sauce and fell in love with go-go music before I even walked on the streets of DC. I found that all people from Atlanta were not ratchet with accents I couldn't understand like those on the reality tv shows (I apologize to my ATL family and friends, those shows did not portray you all well, and I had no other reference!) I was able to truly "explore, discover, and become in Aggieland. I learned who I was and what I wasn't, and I was prepared to become who I am today.

As a Journalism & Mass Communication student, I had the best professors you could ask for. I planned to be a news reporter and an anchor, so I wrestled with shortening my name and perhaps going by Laina rather than what everyone made so complicated to pronounce my entire life: Cheylaina. I'll never forget the encouragement I received from Mrs. Gail Wiggins. She told us to proudly say our full names and to correct anyone who mispronounced it. Dr. Teresa Styles truly loved us as if we were her nieces and nephews. On any given day, you could hear her shouting out "F!" to anyone who answered a question incorrectly. In 2006/2007, blogging wasn't popular, but Dr. Styles introduced us to this new concept and predicted how it would become huge. Years later, I started a wedding blog to coincide with my wedding planning business. It drove sales, placed me in a position as an expert in the wedding industry, and contributed to me having articles published in magazines and on larger platforms. Thanks, Dr. Styles!

When I found out I'd be fulfilling all of my prerequisites for graduation a semester early, I didn't feel ready for the world, so I told Professor Nagatha Tonkins that I was going to graduate school for elementary education as my backup plan. She challenged my mindset when she asked, "Why do you need a plan B if you already have a Plan A? Just stick to the plan."

I was very active during my time on campus; I was a member of the theatre, the sophomore class secretary, interned at the local R&B radio station with Busta Brown (who taught me a lot about radio and often allowed me to co-host the afternoon show with him), and I pledged Alpha Kappa Alpha Sorority, Incorporated. I even finally found my way to Washington, D.C. when I interned in the Creative Services department of Black Entertainment Television. It was a requirement for us to have at least one hands-on internship to graduate. I'm thankful that our department had this requirement because working in the marketing department of BET set me up for my first job out of college in marketing and events, which eventually led me down the path of entrepreneurship and hosting my own talk show/podcast.

Everything I learned at A&T, the relationships I formed, the sisterhood I am a part of, all continue to show up in my life today. Today, at 34 years old, I am a wife and mother of three. But, I wouldn't have these three little HBCU legacies if that one fateful day in 2006 at Williams Cafeteria didn't happen.

My friend Kristen and I would often go to lunch at the cafe in between classes. One day, we met up and, unbeknownst to me, my future husband and father of all of my children were sitting a few seats down from us. Kristen knew him and casually introduced us. He was about to graduate from A&T and head to graduate school. We didn't date in college, but three years later, we met again. We instantly remembered one another from our A&T days. Three years after meeting for the second time, we would marry.

I can't help but wonder how different my life would have been if I chose to attend another institution. Would I have met my husband and had the same beautiful children? What about my career and entrepreneurial journey? Would I have had the same relationships that have connected me over and over again and granted me access through the right doors? I don't know if I would have, but what I know for sure is that all of these things DID happen because of North Carolina Agricultural & Technical State University. Aggie Pride is TRULY Nationwide, and for that I am grateful. I enjoy the life that I have today because of sweet A&T.

About Cheylaina Fultz

Cheylaina Fultz may have been raised as a small-town girl, but she has always had big city dreams with an entrepreneurial spirit, and a passion for acting and media. Since 2012, she has planned weddings and events nationally and internationally. This led her to create The Cheylaina Fultz Talk Show, a podcast that shares stories of women who have overcome challenges and evolved into amazing entrepreneurs and powerful leaders.

In 2020, Cheylaina launched HBCU Legacy Fashion, a boutique of classic HBCU kids clothes that extends the legacy of HBCUs, and increases enrollment rates through her HBCU Legacy Scholarship fund (a nonprofit 501(c)3 that provides monetary support to minority students entering or already enrolled into a black college or university). Because of HBCU Legacy Fashion, more black and brown students will become aware of the possibilities of attending college, and will obtain debt free degrees from an HBCU.

Cheylaina is a proud 2008 graduate of North Carolina A&T State University where she became a member of Alpha Kappa Alpha Sorority, Incorporated, and obtained a degree in Journalism & Mass Communication with a concentration in Journalism & Electronic Media.

Today Cheylaina is a wife and mom of three residing in Columbus, Ohio. She enjoys acting, interviewing new people, emceeing events, and traveling to a beach with a good book in hand.

BRITTNEY DENNIS

Aggie Born, Aggie Bred, and
When I Die, I'll be Aggie Dead
Brittney Dennis

An Educator's redemption tale….

I have attended four elementary schools, two middle schools, and three high schools, but, despite all that transition, the only University to which I applied and from which I graduated with two degrees is the illustrious North Carolina Agricultural and Technical State University.

Born in the "New England state": New Hampshire, Portsmouth specifically. Though I was nearly 800 miles away, there was blue and gold running in my veins. I am one of a dozen Aggies in my family to graduate and find love at North Carolina A&T. I met and married my husband of nine years at the number one HBCU in the World; we gave birth to our, very own, future Aggie in 2015.

By the time I enrolled in high school I attended several homecomings, Aggie Fests, etc… I was convinced that North Carolina A&T was the only university that existed. Matriculating to college was instilled into my brain at such a young age I assumed college was mandated: something like the thirteenth grade. Though the next steps were apparent to me from such a young age, my path wasn't an easy one. My dream school, and projected dream life, would come with major adjustments, sacrifices, wins, and losses.

Education has always played an important role in my family; my mother and extended family instilled in me the value of knowledge at a very young age. However, I always took the road less traveled which resulted in my path to success being a rocky one. My dream was to graduate from North Carolina Agricultural and Technical State University and become a teacher. I only applied to one college: North Carolina Agricultural and Technical State University. You see, dear reader, a high school suspension resulted in NC A&T accepting me on probationary terms. Now, I know what you're thinking: "Why would I do anything to jeopardize being admitted into my dream school?" However, that story is for another book; a story that would take much longer to describe, so let's stay the course.

I had something to prove when I walked onto that campus as an official student during the Fall of 2007. Little did I know that these Aggie buildings, relationships, and life lessons would shape who I am and stay with me for the rest of my life.

The College Prequel:

I was very young, four years old, when my father gained his wings after fighting a year-and-a-half-long battle with cancer. Being a product of a single parent home is one of my greatest accomplishments, but it was also one of my biggest challenges. My mother was an amazing leader and put education on a pedestal so high I would spend a lifetime trying to climb and find it. I observed my mother earn promotions and soar in different positions as a result of her knowledge. So, although I struggled at times socially, school was always my safe place. I attended several schools, but there was always something routine and similar about each one that gave me peace. I had no idea that entering North Carolina A&T would create one of my safest havens known to date.

Freshman Year: Discipline

One's freshman year is the most memorable, yet most pivotal, year of their college career. My one advantage was the certainty I had about my major. I always knew I would work in education, so meeting with my advisor and selecting my study of choice was the easy part; the scheduling and discipline of attending classes wouldn't be quite as easy. I came from a moderately strict home; I partied with curfews and few restrictions, but nothing like the level of freedom college provided. NC A&T provides a real family atmosphere; the good news is: everyone has your back, and the bad news is: everyone has your back.

I found myself missing classes and assignments, and, much to my surprise, like-minded students came to my rescue. They weren't completing work for me, but they made sure to remind me that we were all working toward a common goal. My negligence also led to professors calling my dorm rooms and reminding me of the number of absences I was accumulating. If one was wondering how being distracted from your dream school could be possible, it's not easy to turn down spades tournaments, gym jams, epic snowball fights in the Holland bowl, and the legendary food fight in Willems Cafeteria.

With that said, by midterms, I was forced to shift my focus and surround myself with fewer party friends and more scholars, which, I would learn later, are made equal. My advisor reminded me that to graduate on time, I would need to accumulate enough credit hours each semester; on top of that, to enter the school of education, my GPA must remain above 2.8. Ironically, I managed to escape all my courses with a "C" average or higher except for Biology, this would come back to haunt me in later years, but hey, I was still an Aggie and, at the time, that's all that was important. The Discipline I needed to stay enrolled in was acquired during this year, but the amount of discipline to soar wouldn't surface until much later.

My advisor, who looked like me and wanted me to do well, provided me with two important things: one, it provided a level of accountability that I very much needed; two, it allowed me to dream and imagine a future of success for myself and others.

Sophomore Year: The Shift

By the time I returned to school my sophomore year, commonly mispronounced as: "Southmore" (Aggie Insider), my entire focus shifted. While I spent my Summer in the mall working a part-time job, my peers completed internships or attended summer training to advance their collegiate experience. I realized that my professors had my back, but my potential was being overshadowed by a "Rockstar lifestyle." So, I decided to shift my attire, begin extracurriculars, and most importantly foster better study habits. Aggies are known for partying hard, but they study even harder. I traded my cool Jordan and Nike sneakers in for solid pumps and classy flats, hung up my bodycon and sundresses and invested in shirt and pants suits. To soar, I needed to look at the part, at least on campus and in class. I also learned that I was surrounded by elite Aggies that understood how to party hard while still soaring in class. I had to shift my study groups and expand my networking circle. How does this shift occur? I started with the types of conversations I was having with my peers: which students knew how to access grants, who graduated top of their class in high school, who writes all the papers for group work, etc. (HBCU Insider, if you know you know). Following this, I shifted the conversations I was having with my advisors and professors; I started asking them about their collegiate journeys and describing to them where I saw myself post-graduation.

Immediately following this shift, doors began to open left and right. Professors were reaching out to me about internships and opportunities that would provide me quality experiences for my major. This is the Aggie way; we are a family, but you have to apply yourself first. Remember that discipline I mentioned earlier? Well, as I matriculated into my junior year, the scheduling struggle and Biology class grade will, as promised, return to haunt me. With all those trials that I survived during my two years as an Aggie; I was on my way.

As my sophomore year ended, I met another Aggie, and let's just say that although Aggies often work hard and play harder, we also enjoy finding love; let's just say when I spoke with friends and family, the conversation went a little like: "So, there's this guy."

Junior Year: Senior Prerequisites
Greeks, athletes, class presidents, club members, etc.… These were focused Aggies who were flourishing while also spreading their wings across campus as social butterflies. The members of these

groups are the ones by which I found myself mentored and with whom I networked, traveled, and made post-graduation plans. After all, the dream was to become an Aggie Graduate; however, the resources on how to be successful in your steps post-graduation were slim. I was on course to graduate on time, my advisor who, at this point, was like family, created a schedule that allowed me to take all my courses on Tuesdays and Thursdays; this provided a student like myself more time to study and work a part-time job—partying isn't free... kidding.

So, I was finally on my way. I joined the SNCAE student association for educators; I was inducted to Kappa Delta Pi, an education sorority. Then the internships started and conversations around post-graduation jobs, salaries, and the "real world" were knocking on my door, and suddenly I didn't feel so ready. All my life I had everything mapped out, but I had not considered the possibility of being told no, I should have.

Near the end of my Junior year, I applied for my senior year internship, the opportunity that would shape my life and future career goals. However, I was met with two major dilemmas: the senior internship required a B in biology and a passed Praxis required teacher exam score. I had neither. Changing my major wasn't an option, for I have always had the passion to teach, so my advisor suggested I spend my summer studying for the Praxis Exam and retaking Biology. She offered great advice, she told me: "try going to class, you may learn something." Well, that summer, I spent a lot of time studying, and I finally earned my B in biology as a result I was given an extension on my Praxis exam. Big Senior Energy!

So that guy I met at the end of my Sophomore Year, Newton Dennis, graduated from "this guy" to my boyfriend, and much of his guidance and support helped me focus on what post-graduation could look like for us, and by senior he would pop a question that would change my life forever. The Icing on the cake is that my boyfriend worked with this amazing company called Nxlevel Entertainment.

They threw the most epic and memorable parties ever, so you can imagine how this educator, who likes to party, felt like she was in college heaven.

Senior Year: Graduate or Super Senior

There is no greater excitement, nor stress, than an Aggie's Senior year; you have job possibilities, senior fees, graduation applications, not to mention your everyday college courses which feel as though they hold more weight than one can bear. Well, for me, it was a dream come true; my family couldn't be more proud, my professors were preparing us for job interviews, and discussions on staying local or relocating filled the air. At the beginning of my second semester, I cheered with my peers; "Spring Class of 2011!" I felt unstoppable, but the road I mentioned earlier, the one less traveled, I would journey it once more.

While attempting to submit my graduation application, the Praxis Exam made an appearance once more. By now, I had attempted to pass this exam twice with, obviously, no avail. Now I was looking at adding a semester to my collegiate experience because the school of education couldn't admit me without a passing score. Therefore, my dream was deferred., I clapped and celebrated with my peers who took the Spring stage, and I joined a new study group, becoming a student once more. My classes in the Fall were placed on hold, which was contingent on me passing this test. Yes, my anxiety was through the roof. My family legacy felt like it was in the balance, and I was on the edge of giving up all hope. A major "But God" moment manifested in early August: I finally passed my Praxis Exam, and my graduation application was cleared.

I graduated in the Fall of 2011 with a Bachelor's Degree of Science in Elementary Education, and I later obtained my Masters in School Administration in the Spring of 2020. Right before my second graduation, during the Fall of 2019, I became a member of the First and Finest Alpha Kappa Alpha Sorority, Inc.® initiated into

Sigma Kappa Omega Chapter in Greensboro, North Carolina. In May of 2020, my husband and I paid off $115,000 in student loans leaving us student-debt free. I currently serve as a teacher consultant, with the New Teacher Project partnered with Guilford County Schools. I am a member of the North Carolina Association of Educators; I played a role in two historic teacher walkouts while also serving public schools. Later in my career, I worked alongside NEA, the National Education Association working to recruit, support, and retain new educators at both a local and national level. North Carolina A&T has shaped almost every aspect of the success gained and earned throughout my adult life.

Ironically, I spent a lot of time my first two years being a social butterfly that I failed to notice that shift in my junior and senior years which landed me in the honors section of the commencement program. Yes, little me, a Cum Laude Graduate. If "delayed but not denied" was a book I'm certain I would make the cover. You may also remember that boyfriend that I referenced in semesters passed; during Christmas of my senior year, my boyfriend proposed to me. My beloved University brought me education, friendship, education, a husband of nine years (and many more to come), and, in the Fall of 2012, my education career launched. I was hired as a third-grade teacher in Guilford County Schools and married on August 4, 2012. North Carolina Agricultural and Technical State University and I would cross paths again, years later, and thanks to all the networking when I returned to campus in 2018 I left a COVID graduate in 2020 accomplishing things beyond my wildest dreams.

About Brittney Dennis

Born in the New England state, Portsmouth New Hampshire. I was born with blue and gold running in my veins. I am one of a dozen Aggies in my family to graduate and find love at North Carolina A&T. I met and married my husband of nine years at the number one HBCU in the World, we gave birth to our future Aggie in 2015. I graduated in the Fall of 2011 with Bachelor of Science in Elementary Education and later obtained my Masters in School Administration in the Spring of 2020. Prior to my second graduation, during the Fall of 2019 I became a member of the First and Finest Alpha Kappa Alpha Sorority, Inc.® initiated into Sigma Kappa Omega Chapter in Greensboro, North Carolina. In May of 2020, my husband and I paid off 115,000 in student loans becoming student debt free. I currently serve as a teacher consultant, with the New Teacher Project partnered with Guilford County Schools. I am a member of North Carolina Association of Educators, I played a role in two historic teacher walkouts while also serving public schools. Later in my career I worked alongside NEA, National Education Association in working to recruit, support, and retain new educators at both a local and national level. North Carolina A&T has shaped almost every aspect of the success gained and earned throughout my adult life.

TERRENCE & TAMEKA BROWN

The Crystal Edition of T&T's Love Story
Terrence & Tameka Brown

Fifteen years represent the gift of crystal. It symbolizes the lightness, clarity, and durability of love. 2021 marks 15 years since Terrence and Tameka met and embarked on a long-lasting friendship. Two Aggies found their way to Houston, Texas, in the summer of 2006. Terrence had just finished his sophomore year, a neo of the Beta Epsilon Chapter of Alpha Phi Alpha, ready to have a great summer and make some money. Tameka had just wrapped up her freshman year and was about to embark on her first corporate job as a summer intern. Neither of the two Aggies knew that summer would be the spark to becoming college sweethearts. The two joined about a dozen interns, mostly A&T students, who would be in Houston for the summer working for Hewlett Packard computer company. The experience lived up to every standard set of being the best summer ever. Work hard, play hard, and the rest was history.

For Terrence and Tameka, that summer was the start of a fast-paced friendship turned loved story. Terrence was looking for a best friend which intrigued Tameka as she never really sought out to find her best friend in a guy she was dating. Little did she know, this foundational step would prepare the couple to face all life would throw their way. They were stronger together as lovers, partners, parents, and at the core of it all, each other's best friend.

So, let's rewind a bit…Terrence, a southern gentleman, grew up in a small town called White Plains, Georgia. Terrence was set on North Carolina A&T State University after comparing it to other engineering programs he applied to. One of the main reasons Terrence decided on A&T was the HP scholarship which guaranteed each recipient a personal laptop, tuition, and a summer internship.

Tameka also was granted the HP scholarship and was set on attending North Carolina A&T after visiting campus her senior year of high school. She had locked in every scholarship she could claim, which ended up being a full ride to the university. Hailing from Richmond, Virginia, Tameka was ready to see what college town Greensboro, North Carolina had to offer.

Terrence and Tameka agreed to remain friends after the summer of '06 as they focused on the new school year ahead. They crossed paths often, as they both ran the halls of McNair as College of Engineering students literally from sunup to sundown. From classes, student leadership, working, and Tameka crossing as a Spring 2007 initiate of the Alpha Mu Chapter of Delta Sigma Theta with her 58 AMazing sisters, Terrence and Tameka still found a way to make time for each other. Their friendship grew, and they made it "official" in 2007.

Outside of spending a lot of time together, T&T, as they soon became coined on campus, kept their priorities intact. Then, of course, hardships and minor setbacks hit, as many college students can relate. Still, the two kept each other motivated and uplifted to get through what may have appeared to be some of the roughest moments as collegiate students while dating.

Passing the reigns of leadership of one the most known student organizations in McNair Hall, The National Society of Black Engineers, was by far one of the memorable moments as student leaders on campus for T&T. Terrence served as president for the 2007-2008 school year as he took the reigns from his LB Donald. Tameka got involved early on with NSBE, each year tackling a new position on the executive board. By the start of senior year, after some reassurance she would do great in the position, Tameka ran for president of NSBE her senior year against a friend, aka Mr. Socialite, on campus. This student election between Tameka and Jonathan lived up to the mainstream debates of Barack and Hillary going head-to-head for the Democratic nomination that year. Both candidates rallied in their engineering and non-STEM friends to join NSBE as you had to be a paid member to vote in the organizational by-laws. In the end, Tameka reigned supreme as Madame President with full support from her cheerleader behind the scenes. Terrence, the outgoing president, and boyfriend wanted no part in ruling the outcome of that election, which propelled the organization into a historic chapter year.

Terrence and Tameka agree that their time at A&T was life changing. Fifteen plus years ago, neither of them would imagine that the steps they took ultimately building a strong foundation for themselves as individuals and then as a couple would position them both to this exact moment in their lives today. The friendships cultivated, the richness of A&T's history and traditions, and the dedication they exhibited to excel and graduate twice from the university played a major part in their greatness. That's right, after undergrad, the couple both landed the GEM Fellowship and embarked on yet another new journey, grad school at A&T to get their Master's in Engineering and Master's in Computer Science. What made their success even more profound was that they had achieved something that honestly was rare in their families, which was receiving a college education. They now had the next generation – their brother and sister, nieces and nephews, cousins, and mentees aiming to reach the same level of success, if not higher!

It all started as interns in Houston to the Browns calling Houston their home for the past decade. They continue to be involved in the community, having served as leaders of the Houston Alumni Chapter of the National Society of Black Engineers and navigating the professional side of their respective organizations in and out of the workplace. Terrence and Tameka are still Bigs with the Big Brother Big Sister Program, an organization they were introduced to in college in 2007. The impact they saw that they were making in the lives of two young kids as college students was enough to continue their commitment to the program as professionals when they moved to Houston. Getting rematched in 2014 played a significant role in how the two have crafted their personal time to make an impact in their mentees' lives.

It's mind-blowing to think how much their goals, ambitions, and drive aligned being from opposite sides of the track. As Terrence and Tameka grew closer, they found many similarities in their different upbringings. Their families paralleled in value, structure, and just down-home southern hospitality. Tameka's extended family lived only an hour down the road from Terrence's hometown, which made commuting down 85 South a treat for them both. "Family over Everything" is one pillar Terrence and Tameka keep at the forefront. Being 1000+ miles away from their family and friends is not easy. Still, it makes trips back to the east coast to visit family or reconnect during GHOE so worthwhile. They both agree that family does not have to be blood relatives. Their Aggie family make up a large part of their network of friends that have become family. From HP Scholars to Virginia and Georgia ties, two of the couple's closest friends, Dexter and Sekoya, both Aggies, now reside in Texas and are the godparents of their daughters, Trinity & Tera.

15 years ago, Terrence, 20, and Tameka, 19, found their way thanks to A&T. It has built the foundation for 8 years of a blossoming marriage. Their Faith, Family, Friends, Community, Leadership, Communication, and Love are the pillars of T&T's promise to each other. They keep their mission statement as a constant reminder of their reasons why they continue to strive and move forward. After the heaviness, uncertainty, and tests of resiliency that life and time itself has placed on this couple year fifteen of their commitment is starting to shine bright. Fifteen signifies new beginnings, fresh starts, advancement, mind renewal, re-evaluation, rejuvenation, and remolding. It's crystal clear that these two love birds are destined for success if they can brag on each other just a bit. God orchestrated the way for them to meet as A&T students, and the rest they give all thanks to their Father above for the blessings on top of blessings. Look out world for the Silver and Gold Editions of T&T's Love Story!

About Terrence & Tameka Brown

Terrence and Tameka Brown are double degree holders and proud alumni of North Carolina Agricultural and Technical State University. Graduating with their Bachelor of Science, Terrence obtained an Electrical Engineering degree in 2008 and Tameka obtained a Computer Science degree in 2009. The graduates both received their Master of Science in the same fields respectively in 2010. At A&T, the couple remained committed to their studies while working part-time jobs and being involved on campus. They both have served as president of the A&T chapter of the National Society of Black Engineers and became members of the Beta Epsilon chapter of Alpha Phi Alpha Fraternity in 2006 and the Alpha Mu chapter of Delta Sigma Theta Sorority in 2007 fostering their "BE.AM" love. These college sweethearts found their way to A&T from different hometowns. Terrence grew up in White Plains, Georgia and Tameka hails from Richmond, Virginia. The couple now currently resides in Houston, Texas and have been married for 8 years. Terrence is a Project Manager for Tachus, a growing start-up company and local internet service provider. Before joining Tachus, Terrence started at Walker Engineering as an Electrical Designer and ultimately transitioned to project management after obtaining his Project Management Professional (PMP) certification. Tameka has gained a wealth of global experience working for Shell Oil company for the past 11 years as an IT Business Analyst. She is currently in pursuit of obtaining her Master of Business Administration. In a dual-career home, they are continuously cultivating their marriage to reflect their mission statement to keep God first, foster continuous growth, and be supportive to each other, family, and friends. They've placed a large importance on building their family legacy as proud parents of two diva daughters, Trinity (5) and Tera (2). Terrence and Tameka are mentors to two littles with Big Brothers Big Sisters of America, a non-profit organization whose mission is to inspire children's passions and encourage them to achieve success in life. They have been matched with their littles, Sam and Janea, for the past 7 years and both individuals have become extensions of their family. The dynamic duo, better known as "TnT", are embracing life and keeping the core of their blossoming marriage first which is being each other's best friend.

DEKEVIAS J. "DJ" ATKINSON, SR.

I'm So Glad!
Dekevias J. "DJ" Atkinson, Sr.

My life changed for the better because of North Carolina Agricultural and Technical State University. The brilliant professors, my wife, lifelong friends, and many other Aggies I met along the way are what make me truly mean it when I say: "I'm so glad I went to A&T!" To sum it up, I do not know how my life would have gone if I did not decide to attend the greatest university on Earth.

I was born and raised in Goldsboro, NC. Although my mother and father had a 12th and 10th-grade education respectively, they both had an impeccable work ethic. They also had a desire to do everything they could to ensure that their five children had access to unlimited opportunities. That included either going into the military or going to college to earn a degree. My mother ensured I stayed laser-focused in school. When I was in the fifth grade, I knew that I wanted to go off to college after graduating from high school. From that point on, I used that work ethic I inherited from my parents to get me academically prepared for higher education, and then realized that I was going to be the first person in my household to go off to college and earn a 4-year degree.

I attended Goldsboro High School in Goldsboro, NC. I also marched as a trombone player in the Goldsboro High School Marching Cougar Band, led by former Band Director Mr. Clifton E. Scott, Sr. Mr. Scott was a proud Aggie himself, and he always talked about North Carolina A&T and the Blue and Gold Marching Machine. Mr. Scott was a product of the Blue and Gold Marching Machine, under the leadership of the late Dr. Johnny B. Hodge, Jr., better known as "Doc." My high school band received an invitation to attend A&T's Homecoming in 1992. That year, A&T would play against Bethune-

Cookman College in the Homecoming football game. My high school band had an opportunity to march in the Homecoming parade and perform at Aggie Stadium after the game, as several other high school bands would perform there as well. As a high school freshman, I was stoked to be on a college campus representing my high school and taking everything in that I saw, heard, and learned. It was also the first time I ever visited a historically black college. We were lined up in Holland Bowl, and we were right beside the North Carolina A&T State University Blue and Gold Marching Machine. I remember that Mr. Scott talked at length to this tall man dressed in, what I thought was, a military outfit. Later, I found out that that was how college band directors dressed. It was only after the fact that I learned that Mr. Scott was talking to Dr. Hodge. So, as we were waiting for our turn to step out in the street to perform in the parade, the Blue and Gold Marching Machine cranked up and took off for the parade. I was mesmerized as I watched this all-black, college band high step, play their instruments, and dance in the street. I had already fallen in love with the concept of performing in a marching band; however, when I saw A&T's band at Homecoming in 1992, I was sold. I knew right then that I wanted to go to A&T. I saw myself being a member of that band. The Homecoming parade was overwhelmingly awesome. There were a lot of people that attended the parade, and it reminded me of a huge family reunion. At the time, that was the largest audience for which I had ever performed, and I loved it. The atmosphere was phenomenal, everyone was having a fantastic time, and we then attended the football game. I never saw so many black people in one location like that, but it was like a huge festival. That was the very first time I attended and witnessed what would become GHOE.

During this time, there were other colleges that I was also considering, such as Winston-Salem State University, East Carolina University, and the University of North Carolina at Chapel Hill. I thought long and hard about where I wanted to attend college before making a final decision. However, during this time, my mind always returned to the memory of my freshman year in high school when I saw the Blue and Gold Marching Machine for the very first time, marched in the Homecoming parade, and attended the game between A&T & Bethune-Cookman College.

Finally, in early April 1996, my high school band director, Mr. Scott, scheduled a trip to Greensboro to play in the symphonic band with current band students. This allowed Dr. Hodge to listen to us and see how we blended in with the current students at the time. We also had the opportunity to take a tour of the campus, and I got the impression that every student I saw seemed very happy and satisfied to attend the school. I remember us walking by Haley Hall, and a young lady yelled out of her window "AGGIE PRIDE!" She said it as she meant it. Soon after that trip, I finally made up my mind that I was going to North Carolina Agricultural and Technical State University in the Fall. I was looking forward to band camp, meeting new and different people from all over the state and the country. I was also looking forward to becoming a black man with a college education and the first in my immediate family to achieve such an accomplishment.

As a college student, I had to quickly learn to adapt to a new world. I was literally on my own. I had to get myself up in the morning to go to class; I had to make sure my homework was done; I had to make sure that I was prepared to take those quizzes and exams; I had to juggle between my classes, band activities, and having a little bit of social life. I was also a member of the Iota Zeta Chapter of Kappa Kappa Psi National Honorary Band Fraternity Inc., which is an organization that provides service and leadership to the band. It was at North Carolina A&T State University where I learned the importance of maintaining a balanced life, prioritizing, managing my time well, and staying punctual. Given that I was independent and responsible for myself and my education, I had to decide to do what I had to do with a degree in hand. One thing I appreciated about my alma mater is that the professors were firm but supportive. They wanted to see to it that we succeeded in their classrooms because that meant that we were preparing for the real work within society and in our respective fields.

One of the greatest rewards of attending North Carolina A&T State University is the people I met along the way. I was fortunate to meet my future wife at A&T. I also met people who have become a part of my family. When I think of North Carolina A&T, I think of "family." I already have a very large extended family, so it was easy for me to include some of my fellow Aggie alumni in my large family circle. We grew up together on the yard. These relationships were established in certain entities like the Department of Sociology & Social Work, the Blue & Gold Marching Machine, the Iota Zeta Chapter of Kappa Kappa Psi, the Theta Zeta Chapter of Tau Beta Sigma, and beyond.

One of the proudest moments of my life occurred on May 13, 2000, when I officially became an alumnus of North Carolina Agricultural and Technical State University. It was a wonderful Mother's Day gift I could give to my mother that weekend. I am very proud to say that my attending this world-class university influenced my youngest sister, a nephew, a cousin, and a niece to become Aggies as well. I also have other younger cousins and some great-nieces who are considering going to Aggieland. I knew A&T was something special, and that it has always been destined for greatness among this country's Historically Black Colleges and Universities. There is a reason why it is currently the largest HBCU in the country, as well as a cultural trendsetter. It has become dominant in almost everything from academics to athletics. Its history is second to none. I look forward to witnessing my alma mater make a mark on this society as it continues to prepare young minds for the future. Again, I say I AM SO GLAD I WENT TO A&T!! AGGIE PRIDE!!

About Dekevias Jerell "DJ" Atkinson

Dekevias Jerell "DJ" Atkinson, Sr. was born and raised in Goldsboro, NC. After graduating from high school with honors, he attended North Carolina Agricultural & Technical State University and graduated cum laude in 2000 with a Bachelor of Social Work degree. He attended Howard University in Washington, DC and graduated with a Master of Social Work degree in 2004.

Dekevias is a Licensed Clinical Social Worker in the state of North Carolina, and currently works as a Social Worker with the Durham VA Health Care System in Durham, NC.

Dekevias has been married to Karema Elwood Atkinson for the past 15 years. They are the proud parents of an 11-year-old son, Dekevias Jerell "AJ" Atkinson, Jr, a rising 6th grader. In his spare time, Dekevias enjoys volunteering in the community, traveling, fishing, listening to music and spending quality time with family. Dekevias and his family reside in Raleigh, NC.

DR. GEORGIA SAWYER

A Path Called Pride

Dr. Georgia Sawyer

The Beginning: *Sawyer*

"It doesn't matter where you go for your undergraduate education, but it must be an HBCU." Those were the exact words the first Dr. Sawyer, otherwise known as "Mommy," said to me in my junior year of high school. HBCU: Historically Black Colleges and Universities. The idea of attending college was nothing new to me; however, only attending one that identified as an HBCU was something on which I hadn't fully made a decision. Yet, as time grew closer, the decision solidified, and going to a black college was a journey that I was looking forward to; now I just had to decide which one.

Growing up in rural, northeastern North Carolina, Camden County to be exact, family and pride were not foreign concepts to me. You see, in Camden, if you were a Sawyer, we were probably family. The Sawyer name runs deep in Camden, and the extension of the family has been deeply planted and rooted for many, many years. From kindergarten to Senior Year, I never had to experience a class, sporting event, or any other extra-curricular activity without a sibling or cousin right along with me; that was my normal. I grew up in a place where family reunions were annual, yes ma'am and no ma'am were common language, outside was the bomb.com, switches were real, and porch swings were life. It is through these extensions that I learned what pride is all about, how family sticks together in tough times and how knowing about who you are and from where you come helps to shape the person that you are. And when you're the oldest, you're the one that is held to the highest esteem in making that mark.

The oldest. The first. Numero uno. Me. Now granted, William and Martha hit it out of the park from the start, (shout outs to Sis and Beezy because they hit home runs with you two, too); however, that "oldest" title can be a heavy one to bear. To this day, my sisters got away with things for which I had to beg and plead my dear life and STILL didn't get. Shaking my head. Academics was not something with which you played around in the Sawyer household, especially with my mommy. Any written assignment was always proofread and checked over by the professor extraordinaire herself. I don't use red ink on papers to this day because of those memories. Yet, while she was the guru in the classroom, daddy was the honcho on the court. I was fortunate that I was able to have on and off-court coaches, guiding me through the essays and spelling bees as well as the free-throw forms and fast breaks. If I didn't make the grade I thought I should have, they encouraged and reassured me that it was a lesson and to find areas in which I could have improved. When I didn't make the 7th-grade basketball team, I still believe the coach was angry at himself for that decision, they let me know that I couldn't give up and next year was right around the corner. Yes, being the oldest always had its set of perks and challenges, some imposed upon me, some imposed by my own doing, so it has always been my goal to make my parents proud and show them that what they taught me, I would carry with me. Pride started with them.

So, yes, family and that sense of pride and belonging are and have always been a big thing to me and the one thing that I knew the HBCU that I chose must-have. And herein lies North Carolina Agricultural and Technical State University.

The Middle: *Lucynda*

Ace. That's who he is to me. Always has been… always "Will" be.

Remember, I told you early on that I have done nothing in life without a family member being there along the way? Attending college was no different. A&T couldn't have happened to me without my cousin, William. It's true; as the young folks say now, "no cap." Born eleven days apart, William and I have been "ace boon coons," hence the name "Ace," since birth. Could our bond be attributed to the fact that my mom and his grandmother are sisters AND our grandfathers were brothers? Maybe. Or maybe it's because we have attended school together since Pre-K? Either way, our bond runs deep. Both my parents are HBCU grads and hold doctorates (clearly I had no choice)—mommy is a Norfolk State University (NSU) Spartan and daddy is an Elizabeth City State University (ECSU) Viking, but both NSU and ECSU were "home" for me and "home" was not where I wanted to be. So, though I wasn't unfamiliar with HBCUs, I hadn't been exposed to them all… but it only took one exposure to get me. Will loves the band, and when he showed me a clip of the Blue and Gold Marching Machine, I was sold. Yep, that was all it took. The clip of the band… and knowing that Will wanted to go, too. And when I finally set foot on 1601 E. Market Street to attend a football game, it was a wrap. The clip did it no justice, and I instantaneously felt at home. I applied to a few colleges, but the only one acceptance I was concerned with was A&T. Plus, Will got accepted, so we were A&T bound for sure!

Because Aggies DO all things well, orientation was where it started! A&T has been my home, from the very start. Ms. Denise Iverson-Payne, better known as Ms. DIP, took me under her wing from day one and made sure I knew I was right where I needed to be. Her warmth and care carried me throughout my journey, always reminding me to strive and be my very best; I'm forever grateful. Naturally, Will and I attended orientation together, and A&T allowed me to hone in on my sense of family and pride and allowed it to flourish all the more. If orientation can give me all of that, I know I'm in for the journey of a lifetime.

My middle name, Lucynda, was given to me in honor of my great-grandmother, Lucy. Growing up, that was all my parents called me, and I did not like it at all. Not one bit. And those close to me knew I couldn't stand it. However, the thing about the "middle" of something, it allows you space and an opportunity for growth, introspection, and maturity. A&T gave that to me. From arriving at Morrow Hall to walking across the stage in the Greensboro Coliseum, A&T allowed me to further explore that thing called "pride." I already had a sense of what it was and what it meant when I arrived, but being an Aggie allowed me to further develop that not just in my school, but in myself. Lucynda grew at A&T. When she would see Chancellor James C. Renick (rest well, Chancellor) with his engaging smile and open arms; Dr. Roselle Wilson, in all of her elegance, was becoming more of the student and person that she was meant to be; Dr. Roy Coomans, my academic advisor, was, in the words of the late, great Stuart Scott, "as cool as the other side of the pillow" and pushed me to broaden my horizons in the Biology field; classes with Dr. Doretha Foushee and Dr. Margaret Kanipes made me rethink if Biology and Chemistry were the plans God had for my life, but their push and encouragement gave me what I needed to succeed. Lucynda developed not only in the classroom but through social interactions as well and A&T facilitated it all.

The Award-winning North Carolina Agricultural and Technical State University Fellowship Gospel Choir and the Alpha Mu chapter of Delta Sigma Theta Sorority, Inc., gave me a family. Beginning my freshman year, I became a part of the gospel choir. A&T, for me, is not A&T without Ron Jones and Patricia Wall. Period. And I can't forget at all, Dean Ralph Brown. I owe who I am today, to those individuals. See, that's the thing about being an Aggie, A&T creates a place that gives you long-lasting relationships and people that will forever leave an imprint and impact on your life. The choir brought me joy and gave me strength day in and day out. My faith grew at A&T because of the choir and my sisterhood grew because of the Spring 2005 line of the Alpha Mu chapter of Delta Sigma Theta Sorority, Inc. I know some beautiful, boss-making, authentic women and I am forever indebted to their love.

Lucynda, my middle, is where growth happens, and I am who I am because of A&T.

The End: *Georgia*

I am now Dr. Georgia Sawyer, educated through 3 HBCUs, which started at T. A&T is my foundation, my home, my pride. I've experienced losses and gains, joys and sorrows, yet all are triumphs. I've learned, I've loved, and I have grown because of all that A&T gave me. A&T is a monument indeed.

About Dr. Georgia Sawyer

Dr. Georgia Sawyer, a 2007 graduate of North Carolina A&T, is a native of Camden, North Carolina. Born in Norfolk, Virginia to Rev. Dr. William and Dr. Martha Sawyer, she is the oldest of three girls; Martha, also an A&T alum, and Willette, are truly her best friends.

As a biology major at A&T, she was involved in the award-winning, North Carolina A&T Fellowship Gospel Choir and a Spring 2005 initiate into the Alpha Mu chapter of Delta Sigma Theta Sorority, Inc. Her time at A&T was an experience that she has always cherished and an experience that allowed her to gain not just friends but family.

In 2011, she received her Master's degree in Public Health from Meharry Medical College in Nashville, Tennessee and in 2020, her doctorate in Public Health from Morgan State University. She currently serves as the Director of New Student and Family Programs at North Carolina Central University, guiding incoming students and their families through their on-boarding experience to the University.

JOSEPH T. SHAW III

Explore, Discover, and Become
Joseph T. Shaw III

Attending North Carolina A&T State University was one of the best decisions of my life. I will never forget yelling "AGGIE PRIDE" at freshman orientation. A&T felt like home from the first time I walked on campus as a high school senior on a tour.

I was fortunate to start during the second summer session of 2000. I arrived on campus thrilled to join the Aggie family. My original plan was to walk on the track team; instead, I became a student manager with the football team. Becoming a student manager was probably the second best decision that I made. It opened my eyes to a whole new world. It also came with cool perks such as: traveling with the team, registering for classes early, and receiving some scholarship money. I like to say that I stumbled into the student manager position. Right place, right time. I met one of my lifelong friends, Vaughn, in summer school. We were in swimming class together. We started hanging out and going to Mrs. Winners after class to get a two-piece meal for $2. Vaughn introduced me to his friend, Arnold. One day, while at the Café, Arnold mentioned that he got a job with the football team. The job required him to attend practices and games. I said, "that sounds like a cool job. Let me know if they have any more openings." The next morning at 7 am, Arnold called me and said, "if you still want the job, they have one spot left. Get down here quick!" Little did I know that going down there would shape the direction of my life forever.

I got to the Fieldhouse and met Theron "T-Bone" Thomas. T-Bone was the Head Equipment Manager at A&T. T-Bone gave me a quick tour of the facilities then introduced me to the Head Football Coach, Bill Hayes. The first thing that Coach Hayes said to me was, "we don't believe in walking, everything is on the hop." I didn't know what "on the hop" was, but I knew it wasn't walking.

Being a student manager saved me from having to move off campus. After my freshman year, I entered the lottery system for campus housing; I didn't get selected. I was near the bottom of the waiting list. So, I went to Coach Hayes and asked if he could help me get a room. Coach Hayes made one phone call, and I had a room. Just like that, I was now a resident of Cooper Hall. Cooper Hall was home to the male athletes. At that time, there was no air conditioning in the rooms. During football camp the dorm was so hot, I would take a cold shower before going to bed and then drink cold water to avoid dehydration. This residence hall was a city within a city. You could get the latest CDs and DVDs, haircuts, and whatever else you need in a college student's survival kit without going to the store.

I came to A&T to major in Electronics Technology, but after working as a student manager, I knew I wanted to pursue a career in athletics. I changed my major to Exercise Science. My position and experience as a student manager opened up so many doors for me: I was able to observe sports from a different vantage point; I was able to see professionals assemble collegiate games like a puzzle; I never knew there were so many components to a college football game until I became a student manager.

I kept learning as much as I could in the classroom and on the field. The Spring semester of my Junior year is when I began working with the Greensboro Prowlers Arena football team. The Prowlers played their games at the Greensboro Coliseum, and the team consisted of NFL prospects. I was able to travel to away games, and I had keys to Greensboro Coliseum. In my Senior year, we won the 2003 MEAC Championship in football at Aggie Stadium against Hampton University. That was one of the best feelings in my athletic career. Being a part of a championship team changed my mindset. The MEAC championship ring was a tangible reminder of what teamwork can do.

Going into my senior year, I received job offers from different universities to become the head equipment manager. Aggie Alum, and former Aggie Football Coach, Hornsby Howell recruited me to become the Head Equipment Manager at Shaw University. Coach Howell was the Director of Football Operations at Shaw University while Aggie Alum Alfonza Carter was the Athletic Director. I knew that I would be in good company by working alongside two Aggie Hall of Famers.

I had so many great experiences as a student. One in particular that stands out is when about ten to twelve of us would pile into two cars, late at night, and head to Barber Park to play hide and seek. Barber Park is a public park owned by the City of Greensboro, and it closes at dusk, so we were breaking a lot of rules. One night, while at Barber Park, there was a torrential downpour. We all took off running towards the car in the rain. While running back to the car, Vaughn, who is from NYC, stopped and took off his brand new Timbs then tucked them under his shirt to protect them from the rain. Vaughn then proceeds to beat everyone to the car. I don't know what was more impressive, his lightning speed or his allegiance to preserving his Timbs.

In my Senior year, we won the 2003 MEAC Championship in football at Aggie Stadium against Hampton University. That was one of the best feelings in my athletic career. Being a part of a championship team changed my mindset. The championship ring was a tangible reminder of what teamwork can do.

Who knew going to the library would convert into the ultimate social hour? There is no place like Club Bluford also known as Bluford library. On the outside, it appears as a building of academia where some of the world's greatest stories are told and the greatest lessons are taught. On the inside was the human version of black Twitter before Twitter was a thing. Everything went down in Club Bluford except for studying. Whenever I wanted to study, I would go to McNair Hall which is the home of the engineers.

The beautiful thing about being an Aggie is that Aggies welcomes you from day one. Aggie alumni do not meet strangers when embracing new Aggies. When I was a student at A&T, the Aggie alum that I encountered would always make sure that I was good. Back then, I did not comprehend the magnitude of that gesture.

The student manager job that I started in the Summer of 2000 with the Aggie football team led to positions with Greensboro Prowlers, Shaw University, Northwestern University, Jackson State University, and the Chicago Bears. Starting as a student manager led to me seeing areas of the world that I did not know existed. Explore, discover, become was the motto when I was a student at A&T; I took that motto and applied it to my life. I explored a journey, discovered my calling, and became a better human because of it all.

About Joseph T. Shaw III

Joseph T. Shaw III is an author, fitness coach, podcast host, radio host, and athletic administrator. Joseph was born in Elizabeth City, NC. Joseph is the son of military parents with his father having served in the US Army as an officer ranked as a Major.

While at North Carolina A&T State University, Joseph majored in Exercise Science. Participating in sports and learning fitness has always ranked among Joseph's top loves and achievements. Joseph started working with the A&T Football and Softball teams his freshman year as a student manager. The student manager position at A&T lead to Head Equipment manager positions with the Greensboro Prowlers Arena Football team during his junior year and Shaw University during his senior year while Joseph was still in undergrad.

After graduation, Joseph accepted an internship with the Chicago Bears. Upon completion of the Chicago Bears internship, Joseph worked at Northwestern University as an Equipment Intern in the athletic department. Joseph left Northwestern University and accepted a full time position with the Chicago Bears as an Assistant Equipment Manager. Joseph spent seven years with the Chicago Bears before moving on to Jackson State University in Jackson, MS. At Jackson State University, Joseph served as the Assistant Athletic Director. While at Jackson State University, Joseph mentored students and created a pipeline for HBCU students to get NFL internships. Joseph obtained his Master's Degree in Sports Management from Jackson State University.

Joseph left Jackson State University and moved to Chicago, IL to become a Corporate Wellness Fitness Director. During this period, he was also a Certified Personal Trainer and Nutrition

Coach. As a man of God, Joseph asserts that physical, social, and mental excellence can be achieved by anyone through inspiration, trust, and commitment.

Currently residing in Jacksonville, FL, Joseph is the CEO and Fitness Director of Commit 2 Life Fitness. Joseph has published a book called *My 2 Cents: A Book of Blogs Vol. 1*. Joseph is the host and founder of a podcast called *The Bitter Suite*. Joseph also has a radio show called *The Bitter Suite Quickie*. In his free time, Joseph enjoys traveling, mentoring youth, and performing improv.

OME OF Y'ALL
N'T NEVER
HAD NO
AL JAWN
T SHOWS

The Ideation of my HBCU Experience
Jonathan Rivers

Imagine being 15 years old, at a crossroad in life and your big brother has you visit him at college. This college just happened to be Florida Agricultural and Mechanical University (FAMU) and my brother just so happened to be a member of the Beta Nu chapter of Alpha Phi Alpha Fraternity, Incorporated®. I had no idea what fraternities were all about nor what a Black Fraternity was. On day one he takes me to an auditorium because the "Alphas" are having a program. I'm not excited at all but I attended anyway because I didn't have a choice. About 15 minutes into the program I am getting bored, until Das EFX "Mic Checka" an old rap classic comes on and 20 young men in suits come out of nowhere (something I only wore to church and hated) and start to stroll. The auditorium erupts, the ladies go crazy, they spoke about scholarship, manly deeds, and they all held positions on campus. Most importantly they adopted me, allowing me to stay in the frat house, I had <u>just gained</u> 15 more brothers. On my last day I told a group of my brother's fraternity brothers that I was going to be an Alpha. Being 15 years old at the time, they did the math and said the first time I would possibly be eligible would be in 2006 their "Centennial Year" (100 Year anniversary). They explained that I would be a freshman, and that I should not try to join during such a momentous year. They told me that freshmen weren't allowed to join at most universities. This trip literally changed the course of my life! All of a sudden college was cool and wearing a suit was too. To compound things, my father's younger brother, Dr. Larry E Rivers, was the Dean of History at FAMU, and my first cousin was the SGA President. I had a lot of family prestige at FAMU. So naturally I just knew I was going to FAMU. I also knew getting good grades was essential, and I had to start to apply myself if I was to ever get a chance to attend this type of institution. My GPA went from a 2.3 at 15 to 3.2 by the time I graduated high school. I was the only person from my high school to attend an HBCU but that HBCU would not be FAMU.

My senior year of high school I went to a college fair. My mom was going to take me to visit colleges. I made a list before even attending this fair knowing I was going to end up at FAMU. My short list included Howard, Hampton, Tuskegee and FAMU. My mom told me to select a fifth school to add to my list. I was drawn to this really nice brochure, the school was North Carolina Agricultural and Technical State University (NC A&T). The marketing materials really stood out and it was geographically located on the way to FAMU. I told my mom that NC A&T would be the fifth school on my list.

Our trip started at Howard and I felt like I was still in Philly. I was not impressed at all by its Downtown DC location and I was way too close to home. Hampton was next and they were too up tight, too many rules. Freshmen had to wear dress clothes to class! I thought to myself "NO WAY JOSE!" Next was NC A&T which was one stop away from Tuskegee and then FAMU, my destiny. But when I stepped on A&T's campus it felt magical. The band was practicing marching right through the heart of campus. The cheerleaders were working out running through the campus in what seemed to be slow motion (my high school was an all-male Catholic school and 87% white) so when I saw all that black excellence and beauty I was naturally smitten. Plus the campus was so cutting edge, new buildings, new stadium, it looked like a PWI. During my tour I visited the School of Business (Craig). I had decided I wanted to major in Marketing but my SAT scores would require me to come into school as a general study undeclared major. Which was not ideal as I knew my GPA was solid but I have never been a good test taker. This professor knew I was on my official visit when she saw me walking the hallways of Craig with my mom and she called us in her office. Her name was Dr. Ragon and she was over the marketing department. I told her how I was in love with the school, how my GPA was good but I would have to come in as undecided. We discussed my high school, my family business R Rivers Cleaning company, my athletic achievements, and my mom talked about her scholastic achievements being that she attended Ivy League schools such as: UPenn, Cornell, and Bryn Mawr College. Well Dr. Regan was so impressed with what later I found out was an interview that she made an exception for me and accepted me on the spot into the marketing program. (RIP Dr. Regan I will never forget you and what you did for me).

I turned to my mom at the end of the tour and told her to cancel the rest of my tour at Tuskegee and FAMU. I would be taking my talents to North Carolina A&T!

While at A&T

Upon arrival on campus I knew no one but quickly made friends with people from Philly, Ayinde, Shelton, and Ronshanita, to name a few. I was able to get immediately involved with IMAN Fashions, and even started to promote events and parties with IMAN. I then joined the Student Union Advisory Board (SUAB) as a Co-Chair of the Games & Tournaments Committee, under Ishmail Abdus-Saboor. Ishmail is also from Philly and he would later win a Nobel Peace Prize for his research at University of Pennsylvania.

My freshman year could have ended there. I was super involved in the Student Government and becoming popular on the social scene through IMAN Fashions. But of course I didn't stop there. Think back to when I mentioned my experience at 15 years old at FAMU. I wanted to be an Alpha and it just so happened that Ishmail was a current member of the Alpha Phi Alpha at NC A&T. I formally expressed my interest to him … and the rest is history. Spring 2006 I became a member of the Beta Epsilon (BE.) Chapter of Alpha Phi Alpha Incorporated as a Freshman.

The summer going into my sophomore year I secured my first internship through the INROADS program. Cintas Corporation hired me as an intern. It was a valuable experience waking up at 4 am to be at work by 5 am and home by 3 pm. I can say I learned the most from the veterans and appreciated how much pride they took in providing for their families.

I later became the Chairman of the Games and Tournaments Committee in SUAB. I was the Co-President of Nxlevel Entertainment, the largest entertainment company in the state of North Carolina. I held several positions for the Beta Epsilon. (BE.) Chapter of Alpha Phi Alpha during my four years on the yard including Sargent of Arms, Marketing Chair, Step Team member, Co-Founder of BE. Fit, and ADP (Assistant Dean of Pledging) for the Spring 2009 line of BE. (Rest in Heaven Darius Dawson #3 Spr 2009 BE.).

After A&T
Fall 2009 I graduated with a 2.57 GPA. Not anything to brag about but hey I graduated. I was so involved in undergrad that many times class took a back seat to my activities and organizations. Honestly a sacrifice I would do all over again if I had to. The networking skills, relationships, and experiences I had in college prepared me for life more than any accounting or business law class could.

My GPA and graduating in 2009 landed me working at SPRINT retail after graduation. While others had full time, corporate jobs paying close to 6 figures, Mr. Popular (me) was slaving away at a Sprint retail store back home in Philly to barely make $30k, living with my parents. However, I never lost my way or confidence in knowing that I would land on my feet. Six months later I secured my first corporate job with AT&T in Atlanta. How? By networking. I had transferred to work in Sprint Retail in ATL, upon arrival I started to ask every customer where they worked, and if they were hiring. I would include a copy of my resume in the bag with their receipts! I was hungry and it showed. One customer had a connection with the

Business Sales Leadership Program with AT&T and I was able to leverage that for an interview which landed me the job three months later.

That Sprint retail job in Philly taught me so many valuable lessons and it introduced me to technology which I loved but never knew I had a passion for. Today I have had the pleasure of working for some of the biggest Tech Companies in the world. Salesforce, VMware, SAP, and AWS, to name a few as a Senior Level Consultant for corporations like Chick Fil a, Delta, Home Depot, Mercedes, and Nissan. I have gained so much experience with consulting these companies that I have finally ventured into Entrepreneurship with Real Estate Investing. My company Happy Hour Investors, which I started less than a year ago with my line brother Michael Stanley, is already managing over $1million in assets.

Life has taught me to never give up, it's not about how you start but how you finish. Nothing is ever going to be ideal so you have to truly enjoy the journey. God is my provider not these jobs or schools. What is meant for you will be in HIS timing not yours. I took a road less traveled and still have been successful. I am not done by any means. I look forward to continuing to build my intentional community, and helping others that look like me discover their potential to rise above society's stigmas on our people.

About Jonathan Rivers

Jonathan Rivers born and raised in Yeadon Pa located right outside of Philadelphia PA. He grew up emulating his big brother Raymond Rivers Jr MBA who later attended FAMU and joined Alpha Phi Alpha Incorporated. His mother Nell Rivers retired from Verizon as a Sr. Executive in Human Resources showed him how to navigate Corporate America and the politics it took to be successful. His father Raymond Rivers Sr. was an entrepreneur founding R Rivers Cleaning Co who serviced over 100 retail stores in SE Pennsylvania. Jonathan worked in the family business from the time he was 13 years old and had a front row view of the work and dedication it took to run your own business. Lastly rounding out the tribe that molded Jonathan is his late grandmother Hattie Lockey who was born in 1916 in Marvella Alabama. She was the only living grandparent Jonathan got the honor to spend time with. She taught him lessons on how things used to be for Blacks, how to have a relationship with God, cook, sow, and how to have an unwavering confidence to accomplish anything you set your mind to. To know Jonathan is to know the people who influenced him the most.

Jonathan graduated NCAT Fall 2009 with his BS in Marketing. While at A&T Jonathan was the Games and Tournaments Chair of SUAB. He was a Spring 2006 initiate into the Beta Epsilon. Chapter of Alpha Phi Alpha Fraternity Inc as a freshman, He was also Co-President of Nxlevel Entertainment. Jonathan was also an Inroads Scholar and had internships with Cintas and the FBI during his time in undergrad.

Throughout his 12-year career in technology Jonathan has had the honor of working for some of the top companies in his field, AT&T, VMware, SAP, Salesforce, and currently Amazon Web Services (AWS). He has gained a level of proficiency across a diverse range of industries having consulted companies like Delta, Home Depot, Chick Fila, Nissan, IHG, and the Atlanta Braves to name a few. Jonathan has excelled in a variety of Senior level roles with increased responsibility including employee management, software sales, hardware sales, network consulting, cloud consulting, customer service, billing, implementation, security, staffing, training, retention, and design, His work entailed handling daily operations, managing a team, constructing fortune 5 Companies, selling new solutions and providing excellent customer service.

Entrepreneurship has always been in Jonathan's blood. His most recent business is Happy Hour Investors which is a real estate solutions company located in the Greater Atlanta Area that specializes in buying distressed homes to be rehabilitated to then sell to single families. At Happy Hour Investors Jonathan and his business partner Micheal Stanley (2006 graduate of NC&T, 2006 member A PHI A) find solutions for people who are in the market to buy their next or first investment property, home, or are looking to sell a home or investment property. Their diverse team has experience with all types of buying and selling scenarios, and they understand how to make every transaction simple and stress free. They own and sell their homes, and are confident that they have something to meet the needs of every investor, seller, and buyer.

My Backyard
Leah Billingsley

"I did not want to go to North Carolina A&T State University."

After an opening statement as such, you may wonder why I decided to contribute as an author to a publication highlighting HBCUs. Well, if you are ready for my truth, then allow me to share my story as I take you on my journey to and through Aggie Land.

Growing up in a neighboring city 30 minutes away from the campus of North Carolina Agricultural & Technical State University, the geographical location was not ideal for me. I wanted to go "off" to college, and my definition of "off" was much longer than 30 minutes from my hometown. As a matter of fact, a good start would have been adding another zero at the end of those 30 minutes. I wanted to be further away, living my best independent life. NCA&T is in Greensboro, North Carolina, which I refer to as "my backyard" due to being so close to my home.

I craved autonomy and longed to travel to distant lands. Dreams of fully taking on the world and seeing beyond my current views. After all, Greensboro was like my backyard. Aside from that, I wanted to experience a diversified world that I did not think North Carolina A&T could offer me. I thought attending NCA&T would be no different than going to a family reunion and seeing my family, friends, and loved ones. Obviously, there is nothing wrong with that, but I already knew what that felt like. It felt like eating a bowl of warm peach cobbler. I absolutely love peach cobbler and although it is quite enjoyable, it was all too familiar. I wanted different and to be challenged out of my comfort zone. I wanted to eat the Portuguese dish, Shrimp Mozambique. Something that I never had. It may be delightful to the palate or completely distasteful, but I wanted to try it, good or bad. The huge caveat to all of this was that I did not apply to enough schools to widen my pool of college selections. Considering, A&T was where I was headed.

Once I received the acceptance letter, it was bittersweet. On one side, I was met with a euphoric feeling from being selected. On the opposing end, I was secretly sad to be so close to what I already knew. After hearing the praises of the Department of Agriculture for veterinarian medicine, I decided to accept the offer to join as an Animal Science major. Eventually, I started coming around to the thought of being an Aggie after hearing more about the pre-vet program.

The time had finally come to pack my bags and head "off" on my 30-minute journey to the land of the Aggies. When I arrived at my dorm in the Aggie Suites Building E and found it interesting that it was shaped like the letter "E". If you were to write the letter out, my room was in the center-middle line of the "E". As I entered my room, I was immediately greeted by my roommate and suitemates. I met new students across and down the halls. Students flooding the building excited and ready to start their journey. There was an instantaneous feeling of excitement in the air. If pride had a scent, I promise I smelled it that day. I only wish that I could bottle and sell it because it was a beautiful aroma that everyone should get a chance to smell in their life. That scent dawdled throughout the halls. Being an Aggie was so real and strong that it was hard to put into words. There was no disputing that this was virtuous feeling.

I was officially an Aggie! It was not until later that I truly understood and what that meant. I did not fully realize that at that moment, my life was forever changed. Sounds cliché but it is very accurate.

During my sophomore year, I stayed in the Suites again but moved across the way to Building F. Those Aggie Suites played an integral part in molding me into the woman I am today. The experiences, friendships, and growth during these two years were nothing less than phenomenal. From the all-night study sessions to the dorm parties, I performed a routine balancing act to ensure that I worked hard and rewarded my efforts with fun times with my new friends.

During my junior year, I decided to get an apartment off-campus and embark on a new lifelong journey. That school year, I joined the ladies of Delta Sigma Theta Sorority, Incorporated in the Spring of 2005. This journey opened doors to love and friendships. I met my best friend on my line and she later introduced me to my husband while we were in school. He and I dated in college and now share two beautiful children together.

As a student at NCA&T, you become a part of a long legacy of the civil rights movement with the A&T Four. Taking pictures in front of the "February 1 Monument" devoted to North Carolina A&T added depths and reasoning to the pride felt when I became an Aggie. You quickly learn the significance beyond the feeling that resonated so strongly back in the early dorm days. North Carolina A&T State University is more than college. It is history. A legacy of strong leaders who shaped monumental movements that were felt near and far. There is no wonder that Aggies go out into the world and become great leaders in society. Engineers, doctors, nurses, lawyers, teachers, authors, community leaders, entrepreneurs, professional athletes, business professionals, and the list goes on. There is an honor that comes from being surrounded by greatness. A greatness that rubs off onto those in close contact.

During that same year, I attended a career fair that led to my acceptance of an internship sponsored by MARS Incorporated at the University of Arkansas. That summer, my research was published with the Institute of Food Technology. I became a co-author of scientific research that summer. The following year, I attended the campus career fair held in 2006 and landed my first job offer. I went on to work with the world's largest privately-owned food manufacturing company during that time. This was the first door that went on to open many other doors of opportunities down the road. My published research hoisted my resume to the top of stacks.

Saying yes to an interning opportunity allowed me to build my resume while in college. This mainly worked out for me since I had a change of heart from my original plan of pursuing Veterinarian Medicine after graduating. After working as a Veterinarian Technician for two local animal hospitals while in college, I decided it was not the future career path that I saw for myself.

It is no secret that life throws challenges at us all, and no one person is immune. However, it is in those moments that we discover what we are truly made of. Although we come to college as young adults, we leave completer than we arrived. Equipped with tools of survival that prepare us for future endeavors. At A&T, I learned how to balance life, communicate, work hard, stay focused, and enjoy life's experiences. I get to cherish every memory made and appreciate valuable lessons learned from each of those moments that would help me navigate life after Aggie Land.

So yes, my HBCU felt like eating warm peach cobbler. However, they topped it with the most delicious vanilla bean ice cream. Since I was surrounded by greatness, I learned how to posture myself accordingly. I saw prime examples of black excellence at its best everywhere I turned. I kept up so I would not be left behind. And after graduating, I finally got my Shrimp Mozambique. How, you may ask? Well, my career led to global travels. Because of North Carolina A&T, I got to venture out of my backyard.

Life comes fast, and when I playback those Aggie undergrad memories, I smile. But the best part is that my smile never has an opportunity to fade. I get to reunite with the same people I made those memories with every year at our family reunion. A reunion known by many near and far as GHOE, the absolute Greatest Homecoming On Earth!

In 2002, I became an Aggie. When I left in 2006, I learned what that truly meant. I learned the true meaning of *Aggie Pride*. We are great, and we produce greatness because everyone knows *Aggies Do*.

About Leah Billingsley

Leah Billingsley is a published food science research co-author with numerous years of experience in managing supply chain programs for Fortune 500 companies. Her expertise is in regulatory compliance with specific areas of focus in quality assurance, government regulations, and customs logistics. While working across different government regulated industries, she gained certifications in HACCP (Hazard Analysis Critical Control Points), SQF (Safe Quality Foods), and BRC (British Retail Consortium). Currently, she is in process of obtaining her license as a Customs Broker.

Throughout her career, Leah has built programs to manage processes created to mitigate risks up to $90 million dollars. She has led global corporate acquisition projects of certifying textile manufacturing facilities across Asia, Central America, Caribbean, and the United States to comply with the European originated Oeko-Tex Standard 100 certification.

As a native of High Point, North Carolina, she graduated from the School of Agriculture at North Carolina A&T State University. Although her passion for animals led her to major in Animal Sciences, it was by God's grace and mercy that opened other doors throughout her corporate career. Of her overall achievements, she is most proud to be called a wife, mother of two amazing children (boy and girl), and one pretty handsome brindle boxer puppy.

WILLIAM SAUNDERS

The Evolution of an Aggie
William Saunders

"Dear A&T, dear A&T, a monument indeed!"

These words mean more to me today than ever before, and they have never been more accurate. As an 8th grader, my cousin, an A&T alumnus, took me to my first homecoming in Aggie Land. What an experience! The sights, the sounds, the food, the embodiment of pure blackness were all overwhelming. It was at that moment that I knew where I would attend college Although many used to label A&T as a "party school," and I admit that "The Greatest Homecoming On Earth" did initially attract my thirteen-year-old psyche, it was my research on its academic programs, clubs, and organizations that convinced me that A&T was where I needed to be. My excitement continued to grow as I continued to research and read articles about the amazing work of Aggies all over the world. If you ask anyone who knew me around that time, the *only* school I talked about was A&T. Funny how some things never change! Then, just two short years later, as a 10th grader, my excitement took over, and I applied for admission. You read that correctly. As a *sophomore* in high school, I applied for admission to what later became my alma mater. Some thought I must have been out of my mind, but A&T understood. They sent me a polite rejection letter, admiring my initiative and drive, but asked that I apply as a senior. I was SO proud of that letter because, to me, it made A&T real for me. I showed others as if it were a badge of honor…and it was. I'm sure that letter still resides at my parents' house.

Born in Norfolk, Virginia, and raised in northeastern North Carolina (the "252"), I grew up cognizant of the positive impact and value of HBCUs. Education is a huge priority in my family. I must highlight the power and influence of near and dear Black women in my life—my grandmother, an alumna of Norfolk Polytechnic College (now Norfolk State University), and my mother, an alumna of both Elizabeth City State University and Norfolk State University. So though, as a child, I was not sure what college I would attend, I knew, without hesitation, it would be an HBCU.

"Around thy base with grateful hearts, behold thy students kneel!"

Let's fast forward to my acceptance and first year at A&T; I hit the ground running! There were many exciting events to attend during Welcome Week, and I tried to attend as many as I could. My cousin Georgia and I decided, spontaneously, to sing at a talent show held in Holland Bowl for new students. Seeing and hearing people get excited about us using our gifts on stage was a feeling I will never forget. A&T was a family! This experience led to auditions for the Fellowship Gospel Choir, where I was chosen to join, and began to establish myself on campus. Director Ron Jones and advisors Mr. Ralph "Dean" Brown and Ms. Wall became like parents while I was on campus. I was fortunate to hold positions in the choir, such as tenor section leader and Mr. Gospel Choir. From late-night practices in Harrison Auditorium (before the renovations), the Memorial Student Union, and New Light Baptist Church to engagements and competitions across the state and the east coast, I learned valuable lessons in independence, self-advocacy, conflict resolution, and leadership. Many connections and relationships that were made in "GC" are still flourishing to this day. Additionally, I became actively involved with other clubs and organizations like student government, American Marketing Association, Couture Productions, and the Student Union Advisory Board.

"We bless the power that gave thee birth to help us in our need!"

During my tenure at A&T, I learned how to survive, from losing financial aid to having issues with registration, to being chewed out by Dr. Beryl McEwen and Dean Craig (Willie Deese College of Business and Economics) about my grades, to standing in line outside the Dowdy building demanding my refund check. Through those types of experiences, I learned how to keep accurate records and take care of my personal business as I engaged in what many call the "Aggie Shuffle." As a marketing major, I learned the importance of integrity, professionalism, personal branding, and punctuality. Dr. Jeff Nkonge, Dr. Jacqui Williams, Dr. Beryl McEwen, Dr. Lomo-David, Dr. Snyder, and Dr. Jeff Blodgett are a few of the amazing professors that had the greatest impact on my academic and professional career. They had a way of refusing to allow me to fail. Let me be clear, school was VERY challenging. At that time, I thought accounting, business finance, and microeconomics would be the death of me. Just before my final semester, I had to temporarily withdraw from the university due to family and financial challenges. It was rough! I picked up odd jobs such as fast food, retail, gas station clerk, and automotive sales while preparing for my return.

When the time came, I had a difficult conversation with the then department chair, Dr. Edna Ragins (RIP). She very directly told me if I were allowed to return, I must prove myself and complete each course with flying colors. She knew my potential even more than I did. Thanks to Dr. Ragins and a notable Aggie alumna, Gen. Clara Adams-Ender, who contributed financially so I could afford both summer sessions and books. I was able to complete my degree in December of 2009. I ended my college career on a high note, earning the distinction of being on the Dean's List. I felt it necessary to make those who supported my success proud. They poured into me, and to this day, their words of wisdom and rearing enable me to be successful in my career as a business educator.

"We'll always strive while here on earth, all loyalty to yield!"

As I celebrate over fifteen years in public education, I attribute much of my success and achievement to the foundation and support I received at A&T. Beyond academics, A&T taught me about life and how to contribute to society and my local community in positive ways. As a high school teacher with the New York City Department of Education, I am tasked with helping to shape young minds and help prepare them for post-secondary education and the world of work. My classroom rules and expectations are almost entirely derived from situations and challenges I faced as an undergraduate. Of all of the young people I have worked with and mentored over the years, they are all clear about where I attended college and that I am "Aggie Born, Aggie Bred!" It makes my heart glad to have inspired several of those students to follow in my footsteps and attend A&T.

One particular award, the Dr. Velma Speight Young Alumnus Award, is personally special because I was recognized by the National Alumni Association for my work with up-and-coming Aggies, as an advocate and active alumnus, and my overall career as an educator. It gives me great joy to walk in my purpose and operate within my God-given gifts and talents. A&T has made my life rich, purposeful, and very rewarding. Some of my future goals include opening my own franchise in NYC, completing the Master of Science in School Counseling at A&T, opening a boarding school, and starting a family. I am indebted to A&T, and as an alumnus, I give of my time, talent, and resources as often as I can as an active member of my local alumni chapter, as an Aggie Mentor, and as a member of the Young Alumni Council representing New York and New Jersey. I would not be where or who I am today without the love and encouragement of The North Carolina Agricultural and Technical State University.

Aggie Pride!

About William Saunders

Will Saunders is a veteran educator, mentor, and professional singer. As an educator in urban areas for the past 17 years, he is excited about and dedicated to the achievement and success of the young people he has the privilege of serving. With roles including Business/Marketing teacher, Singing and Songwriting Club advisor, and student advocate, he makes it his mission to mentor and assist students to become wellrounded, responsible, and independent young adults as they transition from high school, to college, and career. As a professional singer, he has supported artists such as H.E.R., Kanye West, Kelly Price, Chance The Rapper, Kirk Franklin, The Dream, Yummy Bingham, Kim Burrell, and others through background vocals. His love of music is apparent in that he plays sounds of different genres, cultures, and backgrounds for students during his classes.

Born in Norfolk, VA and raised in Camden County, NC, Will holds a Bachelor of Science in Marketing, and is currently pursuing the Master of Science in School Counseling degree, both from North Carolina A&T State University. He comes from a family of HBCU graduates as his grandmother, Dorothy, graduated from Norfolk Polytechnic College (now Norfolk State University) and mother, Arelia, graduated from both Elizabeth City State University and Norfolk State University.

Will Saunders is a business teacher at Pathways in Technology Early College High School, P-TECH, an innovative, limited unscreened, 9-14 model school located in the heart of Crown Heights, Brooklyn. Partnered with the New York City Department of Education, New York City College of Technology, and Fortune 500 company IBM, this STEM model program encourages students to pursue college and career readiness while allowing them the opportunity to earn a high school diploma and STEM AAS degree simultaneously. Will teaches the Workplace Learning course to 9th graders, providing the first of many real-world work experience foundations. As 11th graders, students are eligible to apply for paid internships and after completion of their degree, are first in line for jobs at IBM. Of the school's graduates since 2015, many have pursued post-secondary degrees at other institutions, such as North Carolina A&T, and many are currently employed at IBM. What started in Brooklyn in 2011, later visited and endorsed by former President Barack Obama in 2013, is now present in 26 countries with a mission of helping close the gap between young people's ambitions for college and careers and the specific skills needed by employers in high-growth industries. Will is passionate about the success of young people, particularly those of low-income backgrounds. It is his desire to continue helping to provide opportunity and access to students through this "first of its kind" educational experience.

SADE STEPHENSON

The Aggie Legacy: A Prescription for Success
Sade Stephenson

Attending North Carolina A&T State University (N.C.A&T) has been a family tradition for multiple generations in the Stephenson family. My father was the first of nine children to attend the university. My aunts and uncles followed his footsteps. Like my father, many of my aunts and uncles actually met their lifelong spouses at A&T. My parents, who met during their sophomore and junior years, are happily enjoying over 34 years of marriage.

To this day, A&T is a regular topic of discussion at family gatherings with many of us reminiscing about experiences and memories while attending the university. Every year during late summer and early fall, the talk is all about GHOE (the Greatest Homecoming on Earth). In my family, homecoming is just as important as the Christmas holiday. Each year, we discuss the hotel arrangements, flights, tickets to the events and people we look forward to seeing during the homecoming festivities. The three-day weekend is such an important holiday because the friendships that were formed while attending A&T are now a family bond that can't be broken. However, lasting friendships are only one aspect of the Aggie Legacy.

A Dose of Excellence

Another aspect of the Aggie Legacy is one of the institution's core values: Excellence. As a senior in high school, it felt like a natural decision to attend A&T. After all, it was a family legacy and I had been going to annual homecomings in North Carolina and attending out of state games in Maryland and Washington D.C. since I was a kid.

As the oldest of three children and a role model to my younger siblings, I was raised to push and stretch myself to achieve goals higher than the previous generation. The pursuit of excellence was like a torch to be passed on.

If I were to describe the legacy of A&T, naturally I would begin to think of the moments that really changed my life and set the tone for decisions I have made during my adult years.

Diagnosing My Destiny

The hardest decision for me was deciding on a major because I knew I wanted to attend A&T, but I didn't have a clue about which career path I would pursue. At the time, my mother was working the night shift as an ICU nurse in a level 1 trauma center in Baltimore, MD. I became intrigued by nursing because after each shift my mother would share stories about her patients and her co-workers who became my "fairy godmothers" in nursing. I decided to pursue the pre-nursing degree pathway.

An Alternative Course of Treatment

Nursing is a profession I believe has always been a true calling on my life, but my path into nursing wasn't as I had predicted. I did not get accepted into the nursing program during my freshman year, so I changed my major to Sociology. Looking back and reflecting on the moment when I received the notice that I wasn't accepted in the nursing program, I'm glad that it happened. I learned so much about my character and how to overcome obstacles that don't go as planned. However, like a nurse, I realized there was an alternative course of treatment to get the outcome I wanted. During my junior and senior undergraduate years, I continued to take healthcare-related courses because I knew that denial was not going to be my destiny.

I graduated from A&T in 2008 with a degree in Sociology and after graduation I immediately enrolled into the local community college and pursued a degree in Nursing. After graduating with an

Associate's Degree in Nursing in 2009, I immediately pursued the degree I had always planned on achieving. I finally graduated with my Bachelor of Nursing in 2010.

The interesting part is that after completing the multiple nursing programs, I learned life skills that helped me navigate my career path and helped me network with professionals who opened doors for me. With just two years of experience, I became a Traveling Registered Nurse. As a traveling RN, persistence and creativity in problem solving molded me into a master of improvisation; someone who expeditiously evaluates issues and offers viable solutions. I excelled in the fast-paced work environment of the critical care setting. I have worked at large and small hospital centers on the east and west coast in multiple care settings including Post-Anesthesia Care Unit (PACU), Burn, Medical, Surgical, Neuro, Trauma, and Transplant ICUs.

Prescription for Success Includes Challenges

As a lifelong learner, I don't want a day to go by where I don't learn something new. The lessons I've learned while attending N.C. A&T are lessons that I pass on to my patients, students, and my son. I learned to focus on a solution instead of worrying about the problem. I learned how to be proactive instead of reactive. I learned that it is ok to ask for help. I have accepted that asking for help is not weakness; it's an opportunity for growth and mentorship. I learned how to be grateful for the journey instead of focusing on the end result.

I've learned that my journey is unique and I would tell any incoming freshman to be open to every opportunity that presents itself, including the challenges. The challenges are the most rewarding, because the challenges force you to become more confident, fearless, and determined.

Fast forward thirteen years later and it is amazing how life comes full circle. I am currently a nursing faculty member at a School of Nursing, an entrepreneur, and a Nurse Practitioner. Reminiscing on my years at A&T, I would not change a thing. I am grateful for the highs and lows. I am thankful for the denials, and I am thankful for the blessings. I am appreciative of the moments that humbled me and I'm glad they happened.

"My mission in life is not merely to survive, but to thrive;
and to do so with some passion, some compassion, some humor,
and some style… All great achievements require time."
– Maya Angelou

About Sade Stephenson

Sade Stephenson brings more than 14 years of nursing experience and immense passion for educating the next generation of healthcare providers to her role as CEO and Program Director at McKallen Medical Training. She prides herself on mentoring students and offering guidance as they navigate their nursing career paths.

Growing up, Sade thought her career path would be that of a professional dancer. But in college she decided to trade her ballet slippers for a stethoscope and pursue a career in nursing. Following in her mother's footsteps, Sade chose nursing over all other healthcare professions because of the direct bedside experience and personalized care that nurses provide.

A proud Historically Black Colleges and Universities (HBCU) graduate, Sade earned a BA in Sociology from North Carolina AT&T State University and a BS in Nursing from Winston Salem State University.

After nursing school, she obtained a wealth of experience as a traveling nurse, working in the ICUs of world-renowned hospitals like John Hopkins University, Georgetown University Medical Center and University of Maryland, to name a few. Sade continued to hone her craft and even received an award for Outstanding Service Excellence from Wake Forest University Baptist Health.

Sade later applied to graduate school at University of California at Los Angeles on a last-minute whim and to her surprise she was accepted. Today, she is a board-certified nurse practitioner specializing in critical care. She not only holds a Masters of Nursing from UCLA, but also serves as a part-time faculty instructor in the UCLA School of Nursing.

In 2020, Sade was inspired during the COVID-19 pandemic to help with the shortage of nurses and people needing employment. She opened McKallen Medical to train individuals for rewarding entry level healthcare positions.

RENIKA GIBSON

Discovering Pride
Renika Gibson

Attending North Carolina Agricultural and Technical State University gave me pride I could never imagine or even realize I was missing. Pride for my skin, my race, my heritage, my culture, and my being. Growing up, I was taught to hold my head up, speak clearly, and be presentable. My family always reminded me that I have a purpose, and I'm free to pursue it. So, the pride was there, and A&T gave it a whole new meaning.

I will never forget how I got accepted into what I now proudly call my alma mater. Due to a family tragedy and a misunderstanding of the SAT schedule, I only took the SAT exam once. I am not the best test taker. Being preoccupied with a close family member passing resulted in an average test score. I did get accepted to several universities, but I wanted to hear from more, including A&T. While I do not recall how this opportunity came about, I was asked to come and take the ACT exam at NC A&T SU, where I was accepted on the spot! That was the first moment of pride on Aggieland! I was so excited to join the Aggie family like a few influential people in my life. I knew that I wanted to be a business professional or even an entrepreneur who traveled the world and break cultural barriers; therefore, I initially majored in business.

Freshman year was adventurous and eventful. First, I had to find my footing and determined how I wanted to exist in such a large space. Fortunately, one space was not very large on campus, the temporary cafeteria, essentially a doublewide trailer, or maybe two pulled together. However, it was my first intimidating moment. It felt like all eyes are on you as you walk in to grab your tray and eat whatever was decided for you that day. The nerves quickly went away once realizing we were all in the same headspace, just trying to figure it out. And then what felt like a daily occurrence, a food fight, seemed to magically commence. Let me stop, it wasn't daily, but there were a few. Shout out to the beautiful Williams Dining Hall that opened a year or so later.

My first residence was Barbie Hall where I served on committees for activities including seasonal décor, monthly events, and community service efforts. The hall director and staff were super cool and engaging. One moment I will never forget freshman year is returning from my 8:00am class to news images of 9/11. It felt like the world stood still, and we all had to pause with it. After that, the school sprang into action via email, intercom announcements, message boards, and professors to ensure our safety and awareness. It wasn't a happy moment but a real one that I will never forget.

Sophomore year was dedicated to increasing my campus involvement, balancing my studies, and preparing for sorority life. I knew since high school that I wanted to be a Delta. My aunt, whom I look to as a second mom, is a member of Delta Sigma Theta Sorority, Incorporated. A few high school teachers also inspired me. These ladies had an aura about them, an unspoken confidence that demanded space. It was a familiar characteristic that they all exuded despite never meeting each other. But I knew the common denominator was their sisterhood affiliation, and I wanted that. I knew I had to improve my academics and increase my community involvement, which was second nature to me. I was taught "to whom much is given, much is required." It honestly took a village to get me to the place I was and am today. It was understood that no matter the avenue giving back is a must. I joined a few clubs within my major, a committee within the Student Union Advisory Board (SUAB) and was elected Miss Haley Hall. I also attended several Pan-Hellenic events and all the Delta programs because I wanted them to know I was serious. I made sure I signed my name on every sign-in sheet and asked a question or comment during interactive sessions. More to come regarding

Delta. I was becoming a professional student, no longer the newbie on campus.

Things started to get real in my junior year as it became more apparent how close the "real world" was to my front door. I decided to rush up to that front door and made a significant decision to move off-campus with a former freshman suitemate. I was doing the most! Looking back on it, I really couldn't afford to live off-campus, but I couldn't afford to stay on. I do not encourage any students with financial support to move off campus until it is absolutely necessary. It adds another layer of stress to an already stressful situation. I worked full-time, a full-time student, volunteering 8-10 hours a week and still finding time to party. Whew! I'm tired just thinking about it. This part of my life prepared me to be the financially responsible adult I am today, and for that, I have no regrets. At that point in my college career, I realize that this business major was not for me. I couldn't pass that darn statistics class. I had several tough discussions with professors, my advisors, and my family. Finally, I changed my major to Journalism and Mass Communications, concentration in Public Relations, and sprinkled in some marketing electives. While my college pathway was more aligned with my strengths, another semester was added to my graduation date. Eventually, a full year was added due to curriculum changes and class availability. It was devastating at the time but honestly, I needed that because, as I stated, I was doing the most!

I was technically a Junior twice, and for me, the second time was a charm! Life became more routine, and I finally felt like I was flourishing in my studies; finally earning academic accolades. I was interning and learning a little about non-profit, which I decided was not my wheelhouse either. Nevertheless, I learned a few corporate skills, including meeting and email etiquette, networking, time management, and even identifying and addressing workplace sexual harassment.

In 2003, I decided not to apply to become a member of DST with a super heavy heart because I wasn't ready. However, 2005 was my year. As the saying goes…I had my ducks in a row! Pun intended. In spring 2005, the Alpha Mu Chapter of Delta Sigma Theta, Sorority Incorporated received over 500 applicants. I am proud to say I was chosen! Special thanks to my mom, auntie, family, friends, faculty, and staff who all supported me during that time even when they didn't know what was going on. Becoming a member of such an illustrious organization took my college experience to the next level. The Delta journey taught me that I have more to contribute to this world including philanthropy, professional leadership and inspiring the youth. Delta contributed to my drive to break through barriers and obstacles both personal and societal. I can walk into any space knowing that I have the tools to figure out what I don't know. Understanding that I'm not in competition with anyone but myself. Humble enough to ask for help, never forgetting I'm the master of my fate. A good friend always says, "It's not on me; it's in me." I never wanted my letters to define me, but I did take advantage of the spaces and places it allowed me to learn from leaders doing great things in the world.

In my senior year, I did not hesitate to join the Executive Board as the corresponding secretary and served on several committees. I created a short-lived Alpha Mu newsletter. This was the last year of my college career and I was more focused on being an active member of Delta than graduating. In my mind, this was my final chance to be a member at the collegiate level and I wanted to experience it to the fullest. I should have given more attention to my plans after graduation, but it was all about DST. It was hard work and rewarding in ways that help me navigate professionally today.

The "real world" was calling, and ready or not, here I come. I graduated with uncertainty regarding a career, but I knew I had the tools to achieve my next set of goals. To the current students of A&T, let me be clear: I didn't always make responsible decisions and had to quickly find a balance between fun and studies. College provides an opportunity to evolve your life and/or change its direction. Choose wisely, but most of all, never give up! #AggiePride

About Renika Gibson

Renika Gibson has over 14 years' experience in international corporate learning, training and development. Renika is currently a Sr. Instructional Designer leading a team of Instructional Designers on a Grid Modernization project at Duke Energy. Prior to Duke Energy, Renika was an Instructional Specialist for PepsiCo Corporate Finance Division, as well as a Corporate Training Lead at American Express in Fort Lauderdale, Fl. Renika has earned certifications in Project Management Professional (PMP), Diversity, Equity & Inclusion (DEI), virtual training instructor, SAFe 4 Agilist, Product Owner (PO/PM). Renika is a member of various organizations that focus on encouraging minority youth to engage in STEM related career opportunities. She is also a member several professional networks like the International Society of Performance Improvement where members use evidence-based performance improvement research and practices to effect sustainable, measurable results and add value to stakeholders in the private, public, and social sector. Renika started her own training and development consulting firm in 2015 that offers training assets including web courses, instructor-led packages and curriculum design solutions. Renika enjoys volunteering with youth and future leaders, traveling, cooking, spending time with family, fitness, reading, and a recent love for listening to podcast.

BRYANT WILLIAMS

An Educator's Influence
Bryant Williams

My father and grandfather joined the Air Force instead of attending college; my mother received her high school diploma late in life, and I watched as my five older siblings all went from high school directly into the workforce. None of them ever attended college or got a degree. While everyone perceives or measures success differently, and my family is successful, I knew that despite the lack of a family role model I wanted a different path for myself. Yet life for black families, especially in rural regions, can present economic and opportunity challenges. I wasn't sure how to proceed. I found inspiration in perhaps what was an unusual place: TV Sitcoms. I watched and learned about college by watching "*A Different World*" and "*The Cosby Show*", both of which showcased successful black families and their various paths. These television shows gave me the perspective and confidence to chase my dreams. My decision and path to attend college, and to eventually receive a master's degree in Healthcare Administration wasn't easy. I didn't expect it to be a smooth ride, but I did know that if I set my mind to it, I would succeed.

Upon my transfer to North Carolina Agricultural and Technical State University, I was immediately engulfed by the strong and satisfying presence of very accomplished black role models and professionals who were my professors. They were adept and fully engaged in their roles. Even more impactful was that their desired relationship and engagement with me was much more personal than I expected, to the extent that they felt like parents or family more than simply an instructor. They expected not only quality work and effort from me academically, but also personally, in that it became clear I must care not only about my studies, but about myself, my future, and the future of the people in my orbit. They would encourage, support and occasionally scold me, to keep me focused. This interpersonal environment, combined with a very strong and challenging academic curriculum, afforded me opportunities I didn't previously imagine for personal growth. At no time did I feel alone, or overwhelmed. I always knew I would find the bedrock of support I needed to succeed. I genuinely learned to believe in my abilities, to become a leader, and in my future as a scientist.

Of course, given the short attention span prevalent in most any student of this age, there were times when I came distracted or otherwise lost focus. Other times I lost the self-confidence to believe I could or would succeed. It was during these times that my advisor Dr. W. would use his stern, fatherly voice to get me back on track after a poor exam grade or other disappointments. Stern would also suitably morph to wisdom and understanding, such as the instance when I itemized to him the many reasons I felt it was correct for me to drop out a semester. A gentle chuckle and the words, "I'll see you in microbiology class", was exactly the backhanded praise I needed to set me back on course. My professors and advisors were partners with me in my education, and they would simply not entertain any idea of my refusing to overcome obstacles to achieve it.

Not coming from wealth, and like any student, my academic and living expenses were very real. I had the good fortune of an opportunity to work for Mr. Brandon in the microbiology lab, and also to be a research assistant. The obvious short-term goal was to support my need for food, but the experience turned into so much more. For a period, I with the Laboratory Technician and one other student ensured the microbiology laboratories were prepared for the students taking courses. While I had previously taken those courses and benefited from the results of the lab work, I had never given thought to the preparation behind the scenes required to make the labs a success. Imagine my shock when I had to make over 100 agar plates and inoculate liquid bacterial cultures for one microbiology lab class. In retrospect, given multiple simultaneous and conflicting tasks, I'm sure that in first preparation I contaminated some or all of the pure bacterial cultures the students were to use when I was autoclaving other specimens. My work as an assistant wasn't fully behind the scenes, since I was now visible to the students who were taking the courses. Many of them would simply ask me questions, while others would ask for my assistance in performing their lab work, or to tutor them either formally or casually. In retrospect, I view this to be my first real instance with an experience of being an educator, which I embrace to this day.

Of course not all relationships with faculty started smoothly. I do remember Dr. Snell's course in Molecular Biology, which I estimate is responsible for 50% of the grey hair I have today. This course was my first experience with Polymerase Chain Reaction (PCR), and the task was to clone the 18sRNA gene of a cricket. Dr. Snell was new to the University, and over half of the students failed her course making her far less than a campus favorite. All students feared her, and she appeared closed and unapproachable for all intents and purposes. However, as I struggled with the material, especially in communicating my hurdles in writing, I decided I would need to engage with her directly if there was hope. It wasn't without challenges, but it became clear to me that she was misunderstood. Perhaps it was her gothic style, or the intensity with which she conducted the course and demanded results. However, after slow, careful first steps with her, I did in fact find her to be another shiny facet of my experience at NC A&T. I learned that we grew up in the same area, and how much she loved working at our university. We discussed my career path and ideas on how to achieve my goals. Her intensity didn't diminish when she worked individually with me, and she demanded quality. However, I could clearly see that she was a good, misunderstood person only interested in imparting a quality education. Her style was unique, but she forced me to really dig deep in research and work ethic. She took the time to understand my challenges in writing, and offered extra energy to ensure I wrote my lab reports correctly. She made me work and she wasn't willing to compromise on quality, but I believe that my greeting her with a smile each day, plus getting to know her as a person, made a difference for us both in our roles. My experiences with her helped shape how I perform today as an educator. It makes me sensitive to how students perceive me and my teaching style, and informs me that I must find ways to break through false perceptions of students to always find a way to make them successful. While my students today are certainly adding to my grey hair, I embrace the reality that I can learn from my students as they learn from me.

When my daughter, Brooklynn, makes her decision to attend college. I hope that she will be an Aggie. I've learned other universities just don't ignite the sense of pride and the value of hard work in their students like you've read in my excerpt. My relationships with the professors, staff, and other students left a lasting impression on my time at NC A&T. Each day that I teach, I thank God that I'm an Aggie. NC A&T is more than just a Black College in America. It is a place to foster a community and to develop all your unknown talents. For me, NC A&T molded a passion for educating in the sciences and best of all, gave me a family that I can always call on.

About Bryant Williams

Bryant Williams is an educator in the Gwinnett County Public Schools system in Lawrenceville, Georgia.

Bryant's experiences in educational systems have made it clear for him how caring educators create positive change and impart optimism. In his personal as well as in his professional life, his goal is not merely to disseminate information for memorization and regurgitation, but to provoke greater pursuit and learning. As such, he is continuously drawn to roles and situations where he has the opportunity to lead, and motivate both students and colleagues in the learning process. He has excelled at providing instruction in special education science, robotics, English language arts, and physical science. Bryant is an educator at heart.

Bryant was granted BS in Biology from North Carolina Agricultural and Technical State University, and a MS in Healthcare Administration. Applying his experiences of science and teaching, Bryant created a tutoring program focusing on science for my fraternity Alpha Phi Alpha Fraternity Inc.®, Nu Mu Lambda Chapter, for the young men in the mentoring program. Bryant's future personal and professional path is to complete a PhD program in education administration and policy, which he will apply to advocate for and create educational systems focused on the betterment of K-12 education, especially in minority communities.

When not challenging his mind, he enjoys challenging his body with a daily fitness routine, playing rugby, and shredding the slopes of Big Mountain in Montana with a broad quiver of snowboards. The most enjoyable and greatest achievements of his life are his family and beautiful daughter.

CHRISTINA CALDWELL, PE

Aggie Spirit: It's Good Enough for Me
Christina Caldwell, PE

The world is just coming around to understand the talent, the reach, and the culture that comes out of North Carolina Agricultural and Technical State University. As for me, though, I was born into its richness. My mother, Elaine Morrisey (C/O 1977), met my father her first week as a freshman at Aggieland. Both of my mother's sisters, a brother, and sisters on my father's side are all Aggies. My aunt, Pauline Brown (C/O 1970), met my uncle while living in Greensboro after graduating from A&T. Aggie Pride is generational for me. Much like anything that makes an impact in life, I had to come to know and love A&T for myself and let me say with all certainty, attending A&T was one of the best decisions of my life.

My father, Romeo Morrisey (C/O 1976), is a retired Colonel in the United States Army. Even though I have many family members who attended A&T, I was not provided the opportunity to grow up in Greensboro or physically with the people who were also Aggies due to my dad's career. However, the lifelong ties to the school still made their way to portions of my life. The first truth I was introduced to was seeing firsthand that Aggies attend A&T and then want to give back. We lived in Greensboro for a stint while my dad taught in the ROTC program. The same program afforded him, one of ten siblings, the opportunity to attend college and launched his military career. My uncle, Ralph Brown (C/O 1975), worked at the university as Dean of Students for decades and was involved with the football team where he also once played. My aunt, Christine Evans (C/O 1969), worked in A&T's financial aid office for years. My sister, cousins, and I sent dozens of our friends and associates to see our "Aunt Chris" over the years.

We knew she would do everything in her power to help students find the finances to stay and complete college, especially for her beloved alma mater. My family members serve this country and are business professionals, healthcare workers, educators, HR professionals, social workers, and engineers. Confidently, we can work anywhere and do anything. My family chooses to give back to the university that has given so much to us. Seeing this evidence in my childhood and through adulthood always made me feel proud and hopeful to have a similar opportunity to give. Eventually, my career brought me back to my alma mater. I am honored to be the electrical engineer of record for the newest building addition to the campus, the ERIC (Engineering Research and Innovation Complex) building. I joined an engineering firm that turned out to be the mechanical/electrical/plumbing designers for quite a few projects on campus. In joining, I was able to see the construction of the new engineering building from start to finish, and I get to continue to work on upcoming projects throughout the campus. Honor and privilege do not entirely give justice to what I feel for my university. I am afforded to give back to my university, which makes me very proud that the place that started my career is also a place where I can continue my profession.

For many years of my youth, I wanted to be an architect. Several programs around the country had prominent architecture programs. Although I was introduced to North Carolina Agricultural and Technical State University through my family's stories, I focused more on the universities known for producing architects. In high school, I decided that I was more interested in architectural engineering than architecture. With this change in interest, the next essential truth that I was introduced to was the strong and world-renowned engineering programs at A&T. A&T produced astronauts, doctors of philosophy in engineering, engineers, and many other professionals out of McNair Hall.

Most importantly, for me, the university had one of the very few and select architectural engineering programs in the country. Today, I'm an electrical engineer by trade and licensing. Because of my education through the architectural engineering program, I was introduced to various disciplines. Joining the construction industry, I am armed with knowledge in mechanical, plumbing, fire protection, structural and architecture, in addition to electrical engineering for construction. I have a unique understanding of some knowledge across different trades, allowing me to move quickly into project management positions and teach on the collegiate level. I cannot say I would have been given the same skillset had I gone anywhere else. I can say that my alma mater prepared me for both my career and beyond.

Years departed from my college experience, and the most profound truth, for me, is that there is nothing better than an education from a Historically Black College and/or University. As a military brat, I moved around quite a bit. I was able to witness and interact with different cultures and races, as well as live in various locations. My childhood and friends were my own personal melting pot. Everywhere I lived, I came to realize that those experiences are not always common. A lot of people live in the same place and see the same types of people. And in corporate America, engineering specifically, there has been a history of a stark lack of diversity. Attending A&T was the only time in my life that I was purposefully and willfully among the array of people that looked like me. Yet, there were still so many different backgrounds, cultures, and much to learn about myself. My collegiate experience at an HBCU was a safe space for me to enter adulthood, unapologetic in discovering who I was and confident in who I would grow to be. I was surrounded by people preparing for a corporate world or profession not often thought to include Black people. We all believed that we could complete a degree and go into the working world to succeed in these non-diverse areas. We all were at this university to do just that. We studied together, tested together, and graduated together.

We were hopeful that we would go out into the working world and not be bound by our race. A&T gave me the confidence to walk into rooms where no one looked like me, knowing that there were people with the same career interests as mine in the world. Even if it was not represented in the room. A&T made sure I was prepared, knew that I was enough, and called me to work to earn every space I would be in.

I made lifelong friends at North Carolina Agricultural and Technical State University. From other architectural engineering majors, connecting with people from the different cities to holding leadership positions in organizing and pledging through the Alpha Mu chapter of Delta Sigma Theta Sorority, Incorporated. Also, I could share some time at the university with my older sister, older cousins, and younger cousin. No group of people yells "Aggie Pride" louder than we do. I have a support system of people who are now mentors, sounding boards, think tanks, and business partners. I share in the passing of stories with my parents, cousins, and a host of uncles and aunts who are fellow Aggies. The Aggie Pride permeates throughout different areas of my life. When I think about my alma mater, the thoughts are accompanied by nothing but pride. That Old Aggie Spirit is, indeed, good enough for me.

About Christina Caldwell, PE

Christina Caldwell, PE is a professional engineer, a project manager at an engineering consulting firm and author of "Knowns, Unknowns, Solutions." Having an interest in writing from a young age and feeling the pull to share experience, Christina compiled the memories of pivotal moments in her career and organically turned it into a book. After obtaining a Bachelor of Science degree in Architectural Engineering and a Master of Science degree in Civil Engineering, she began her unique journey in the construction industry and became a licensed professional engineer in Power. This career did not afford her an abundance of representation, so the passage to licensing, management and partial ownership was often one of trial and error. The rewards and learning experience have proven worthwhile for this wife and mother of two. As she continues her career in engineering, she feels motivated to showcase women and women of color who have successfully navigated careers that are not filled with people in boardrooms with the same culture or backgrounds. She, along with and supported by others, are not just engineers but engHERneered.

CANISHA CIERRA TURNER

The Big Fish
Canisha Cierra Turner

"We love you. Take care of yourself," my parents urged after we'd just finished setting up my dorm room and they prepared to head back to Virginia. I remember seeing that green Dodge Crysler van driving away making a loop around what was then Bluford Circle. It seemed like the scene from a movie where the slow, heart wrenching music began to play. It was at that moment that I knew that my life was about to change.

Growing up, my parents always made sure that my big brother and I had the best, were exposed to experiences, and knew that there was a big world outside of Sussex County. They worked day in and day out to ensure that we had the best shot of getting out. But, of course, coming from a rural country town, that meant "you made it". The goal was to only come back for family reunions and holidays— and you better come back successful according to my daddy. He looked forward to always being able to dote on me at family functions saying, "Yeah, my baby is doing great! She's at North Carolina A&T doing big things! Student Government, straight A's, internships, everything. She's a star."

And we can't forget the chime in from my sweet, supportive Momma, "Yes, and she said she definitely doesn't want to come back around here. No grass will grow under her feet!" I was their prize and they flaunted it whenever they wanted to.

Let's not forget my big brother whose heels I stayed from the time that I was a little girl. Typical sibling rivalry, but I constantly heard stories from his friends of how much my brother bragged on his little sister. "Yeah man, she's something else. Something special." He is ten years and four months my senior and he gave me a glimpse into what was to come. I definitely have to credit him for my decision to attend North Carolina A&T.

He surprised me my junior year of high school with concert tickets to the Jennifer Hudson and Robin Thicke concert. After the concert, he said, "I want to show you something. Just sit back and ride." I remember him circling me around the beautiful campus of A&T. He then prophetically said, "I can see you here."

See my brother is my best friend. I remember all his stories of his time at Virginia State University—marching band, pledging a fraternity, amazing mentors, and so much more. I knew I wanted that same experience, just bigger and better.

August 2010 was such a defining moment for me. New Student Orientation. I remember lying in Aggie Suites F while my parents were at the hotel. I recollect lying there thinking, "Wow, I'm about to do this. I know no one. I am the only one from my high school who went to A&T. I don't have any family in Greensboro. I have to start from the bottom again and become a little fish in a big pond, where I once was a big fish in a small pond at Sussex Central High School. Is college going to be hard? Can I kiss my straight A's good-bye? Will people know me?" I mean, everything you could imagine was running through my head. The following day, I attended the first orientation session and got a taste of what my next four years would look like. Anxious, but vowing to not let anyone see me sweat, I just tapped into who I was and what kept me on top in high school. "Just shine, Canisha. Do what you know how to do. Overachieve." So, I sat in the front at all the sessions and took notes.

I remember one session in particular when the Student Government Association came and introduced themselves. That's when I heard the then SGA President, Wayne Kimball, Jr. speak for the first time. I thought, "This guy is amazing. Wow, I think I can do that." I then saw Miss A&T, Carla Saunders, and Mister A&T, Todd Porter. "I can do that, too," I thought. These three people amazed me so much—and scared me at the same time. At that moment I truly knew that I was indeed a "small fish in a big pond." I saw thousands of other Canisha's at orientation and current students who were incredible. Oh my God, how can I compete? How can I create a name for myself in this big place? Well, leave it to my daddy to ensure that would happen quick, fast, and in a hurry. The last session came, and I remember this faculty member tapping me on the shoulder and asking if my name was Canisha. I said, "Yes, sir. Is everything okay?"

His only reply was, "Come with me."

OMG! What had I done? I was going back and forth in my mind, wracking my brain to see if I remember doing something wrong in any of the sessions. Then, finally, I got to the back of the stage, and the gentleman said, "We need a student to give a synopsis of the weekend for the closing ceremony. I met your dad in the hallway, and he said you could do it."

Smh … Daddy strikes again! Now how in the world did he get into this guy's ear?

The Account According to my Daddy:

After being in all those parent sessions, I was tired the entire weekend that I stole away to a corner in a hallway and took a nap. The next thing I know, I remember waking up to this guy coming down the hallway talking. He just randomly stopped me and asked if I had an incoming freshman at orientation this weekend. I told him "Yes." He said that he needed a student to recap the weekend and asked if I thought my child would want to do it. I hopped up so quick and said, "Absolutely! If you give my daughter a microphone, she'll light it up." So, I ran to get your momma and asked where you were. She told me you were in a session. I gave the guy your name and he said he would get you before the ceremony starts…so that's how that came to be.

Call it destiny. Call it my daddy being at the right place at the right time. Call it my daddy being Daddy and always being my biggest advocate. Call it whatever you want, but it was at that orientation that all my worries went away. All the questions I had were answered after a simple encounter with my daddy and Jasmine McInnis. Fast forward to three minutes before I had to go onstage at Corbett Sports Center. No prep, no notes, no nothing. I grabbed the microphone and I spoke. Surprisingly, I received a standing ovation. After I got offstage, I remember Wayne, Dr. Rashid, Chancellor Martin, and so many other people coming up to me saying how awesome I'd done. Then, I remember Jasmine McInnis prophetically saying, "You're going to be our SGA President in four years."

I was on my way to becoming a big fish.

I have so many fond memories of my time on the hallowed grounds of North Carolina A&T. I honestly could write for days on my time there, the incredible people I met, and even the lives I've been able to touch. But, were my four years all roses? Of course not, and some of those fears that loomed my head at orientation resurfaced, but I'm so thankful to God that I always went back to the core of who I was. My parents and my big brother were the motivation for everything I did. Nights I cried, I thought of my parents, and I pushed. The days when I questioned my intelligence in Professor Hayes' English Class (she was super hard on me for good reasons) or was tried to my whit's end in Dr. Phillip's Accounting Class, I pushed. When I pledged the Alpha Phi Chapter of Alpha Kappa Alpha Sorority, Incorporated all while being Vice-President of Internal Affairs in SGA and running for SGA President the following spring, I pushed. When friendships were tested and I found out what I was truly made of, I pushed. I pushed. I prayed. I persevered.

One of my fondest moments was leading over ten thousand students as the SGA President. I met so many incredible people who are now my best friends. The labor was hard, but the rewards were plentiful. I sacrificed a lot as one of few female SGA Presidents.

Some of the things that the men were able to do, I couldn't as a woman. I was in a fishbowl and my every move was watched and analyzed. However, the things I was able to accomplish outweighed them all. I often think back to board of trustee meetings, city rallies, revamping the SGA constitution, voter registrations, the infamous tree lighting that has a story of its own, the Black History Club shenanigans, the A&T Register 21 Questions, SGA trips, studying abroad in Ghana, West Africa and so much more. I am grateful for the opportunity to form connections with the likes of Jesse Jackson and so many other prominent celebrities. I also can't forget braving the snowstorm to stay with the honorable Andrew Young and Omarosa at the Marriott downtown after they invited my board to their hotel room. Boy will that forever be a night that I will never forget. Each and every one of those encounters shaped me into the person I am today.

I often think back to that little girl at orientation. So scared, but filled with so much wonder and potential, she had no idea the impact she would make. Her only goal was to establish her name and boy did she do just that and much more. She allowed her heart to guide her, and she remained true to herself and her roots.

I received this sweet message from one of my mentees and best friend a couple of months ago:

"Nish, I don't tell you this enough, but I still owe a lot to you... being my mom, big sis, and mentor in college has shaped me so much into the man I am today and what I want out of life. So, thank you for always being there."

To me, all of this is the art of "making it or becoming the big fish"—helping to create other big fish. I honestly think that is my greatest treasure left at North Carolina A&T: the numerous lives I was able to touch and those who touched mine. North Carolina A&T gave me so much. It gave me a sense of belonging and taught me exactly who I was and what I was called to be. It was one of my inspirations for my business, Executive Reign, and so much more. I am forever indebted to such a magnitude of university and will always pay homage to the institution who introduced me to myself.

Because of it, this fish continues to swim.

About Canisha Cierra Turner

Born with the gift of speech wrapped up in a heart of love since the age of 2 years old, Canisha Cierra Turner is the true definition of extraordinary. She is a marketing and sales powerhouse by day, and a business owner and prolific speaker by night. She is the Owner and CEO of Executive Reign—a pageantry, leadership development, and talent management company based in North Carolina but serves multiple states. Canisha Cierra has had the pleasure of training some of the most talented and brightest rising stars across Southeastern United States. She has trained Local, State, National, and International pageant winners from 0 to 30+ years old in a reputable portfolio of pageant systems. Her success as a pageant coach and talent manager comes from her diverse background in scholarship pageants, natural pageants, semi-glitz pageants, theater, and of course, motivational speaking. Several of her Executive Reign clients have walked in New York Fashion Week, casted for several national projects, booked commercial and print work, and have become successful Kidpreneurs.

In 2011, Canisha Cierra's national and international service work was nationally recognized by superstar Janet Jackson for the 2011 Janet Jackson 20under20 Extraordinary Youth Award in Atlantic City, New Jersey. She was honored personally by the celebrity and her staff. Because service is a high priority for her, Canisha Cierra has traveled to Ghana, West Africa to donate books and speak to village schools in Kumasi, Ho, Accra, Elmina, and Cape Coast. She did all of this during her undergraduate career as the 2013-2014 Student Government Association President of North Carolina A&T State University.

Canisha Cierra has spoken to audiences all over the United States of America as a motivational speaker. Her speeches are inspirational, thus encouraging audiences to think, "Who Am I Not to Be?" She brilliantly crafts motivational messages intertwined with modern and historical real-world examples to match whatever the theme of the event. From the youngest audience member all the way to the oldest, she leaves each audience member inspired and charged to conquer the world. Canisha Cierra has spoken alongside greats such as Jeff Johnson, the honorable Andrew Young, Omarosa, Malik Yoba, Tatyana M. Ali, Jesse Jackson, and several others. She has also published several articles including, We Speak Your Names, which pays homage to the women of the civil rights movement. She has also been nationally recognized as Wednesday's Woman of the Week by The SBB Institute for the Development of Women Leaders.

Canisha Cierra serves on several boards including the North Carolina A&T State University's Alumni Convention Board, Queen in You Board of Directors, and several other community organizations. She was also named one of the Top 10 Women Entrepreneurs to watch in 2018 by social blogger, Marcia Lindsey. She holds a Bachelors degree from North Carolina A&T State University and a Masters Degree from Wake Forest University. She is a member of Alpha Kappa Alpha Sorority, Incorporated.

Finding My Way Home
LaRia B. Land

I was introduced to my beloved North Carolina Agricultural and Technical State University (NCA&T) through a nonprofit called Target H.O.P.E. just before my senior year – circa 2007. Based in Chicago, Illinois, this organization provides academic support and other resources to Black and Brown students as they matriculate through high school, including rigorous assistance during the college application process.

You see, I was a typical smart Black girl growing up on Chicago's Southside. I was an honor roll student, cheerleader, and newspaper and yearbook journalist at an elite high school, who also held a part-time job. My grandparents and mother raised my seven siblings and me in what was once a thriving working-class neighborhood. While my neighborhood wasn't on a full downward spiral like other majority Black communities at the time, it was laced with all the stereotypes of inner-city life. So, from a very early age, I knew that graduating from a top university was my best chance at making sure my family and I had a bright future. That made me adamant about keeping my grades high and starting my college research early. I viewed college as an opportunity to go out and experience all that the world had to offer. I would have a bit of relief from my family pressures and responsibilities, and the freedom to develop who I wanted to be. So, I finished my junior year with a wish list of colleges I thought would be best for me. This list was based predominantly on advice from relatives who had attended predominantly white institutions (PWIs). I never thought I needed to visit these schools to make my decision, partly because I knew my family did not have the time or money to spare. I decided I would just figure it out when I got accepted.

As you probably expected, I was completely wrong!

I don't recall who recommended me for Target H.O.P.E.'s summer college tour but I am incredibly grateful that they did. Over the course of a week, a bus full of rowdy teenagers hit the road to visit several Historically Black Colleges and Universities (HBCUs), and a few PWIs that had had significant support for minority students. Those stops included Howard University, Hampton University, North Carolina A&T State University, Tennessee State University, Fisk University, the University of Missouri at Columbia, the University of Maryland, College Park, and Washington University in St. Louis.

Before this tour, I only vaguely knew about most of these schools. In Chicago, I was hundreds of miles from the closest HBCU, and as a student of the public school system I was pushed to attend my own state's flagship schools. Additionally, I had adults in my life that felt like choosing an HBCU was settling, and at the time, I wasn't equipped to disagree with them. The thought of out-of-state tuition alone was enough to give me hives and I couldn't imagine what it would have been like to live in a rural town. Ultimately, it felt like attending an HBCU was a dream I did not have the luxury of dreaming.

Again, I have never been so grateful to be wrong!

I often refer to Target H.O.P.E. as the gold standard of college touring because this tour helped me to imagine "me" on those campuses in the most authentic way. I could envision myself not just as a student, but as a smart, Black young woman from a major city hundreds of miles away. By talking with actual students and alumni from Chicago it confirmed for me that I could come from a single-parent family, with limited scholarship money and familial financial assistance, and thrive on a campus that was more than a few hours drive from home.

There were great things about each university I visited, but none of them compared to the illustrious North Carolina Agricultural and

Technical State University. Our trip to campus was perfectly timed because classes were in session. Our tour guide was an alum who flew to North Carolina from Iowa where he worked as an engineer at the world's largest food & beverage company. First up was an admissions presentation where we turned in applications and would learn before the end of our visit if we were accepted. We got to see actual class sizes, dorms, and meet with administrative staff like the Provost. I'll never forget our guide encouraging us to build relationships with senior administration just as we had in high school. We ate at Williams Cafeteria, aka the Caf, toured the museum on campus, took photos in front of the A&T Four statue, hung out in the student union, and raided the bookstore. In true Mr. Williamson fashion, he walked up to random students and asked them to tell us about their experiences, which they eagerly did. Our tour guide showed us his favorite hangout spots, gave us tips on how he connected with his professors, and several strategies for successfully living so far from home. I will never forget how I felt when we returned to the admissions office that day and I was among the students accepted on the spot!

I could rave about how comprehensive and engaging the tour was, but we all know the phrase that sums it up – Aggie Pride! It isn't something that can be truly described, it must be experienced. I heard it in our tour guide's voice as he recounted the depth of the alumni network. I saw it on the faces of the students, no matter if they were debating their professors in class or hanging out in front of the Caf. I felt it as I walked the campus, learning about the Aggies who made and are making history. That day, I realized that if I was going to leave the only home I had ever known, it had to be for more. I had to make a choice that was for more than academics, more than some legendary parties, and more than a respectable name for my resume. So, I traded in one home, for another.

That is what North Carolina Agricultural and Technical State University is to me. It is home. It is where I truly began to learn who

I was and what I stood for. NC A&T is where I learned to fight for myself, my goals, my dreams, and my community. From being an Orientation Student Leader and Student Senator for the College of Arts and Sciences to traveling abroad with the Honors Program and writing for the award-winning A&T Register, I learned what I was passionate about and how to be a leader. The NC A&T family is second-to none and I can't imagine belonging to any other.

About LaRia B. Land

LaRia B. Land graduated from North Carolina Agricultural and Technical State University in 2012 with a B.S. in Journalism and Mass Communication. She later earned her M.P.S. in Public Relations and Corporate Communications from Georgetown University.

A dedicated Communications strategist, LaRia has spent nearly 10 years helping nonprofits, small businesses, and government agencies tell their stories and make meaningful connections with their audiences. Currently she serves as the Digital Communications Manager for a government agency in Maryland.

When LaRia is not cultivating digital strategies, the Chicago native is volunteering with organizations that support and nurture the growth and success of women and girls. Recent affiliations include the YWCA and Lynn's Gift, a Chicago-based nonprofit.

Currently, LaRia resides in the Washington D.C. metropolitan area with her dog, Winston.

DR. JANET WHEELER

A&T: Vision to Reality
Dr. Janet Wheeler

I grew up in the Southside of Chicago. Yes, the same place that's often portrayed in a negative light in the media. Chicago is rather segregated, with high poverty and crime rates, but there are two sides to every coin. The other, more positive, side about growing up in a segregated community is that you don't have to look far to see examples of Black Excellence.

My grandfathers were both an integral part of building Black-owned companies in Chicago's historic Bronzeville community. My paternal grandfather, Lloyd G. Wheeler worked his way up from being a mailroom assistant to becoming the President of Supreme Life Insurance Company. My maternal grandfather, J. Mark Britton, migrated from Alabama to Chicago in the 1930s after graduating from Miles College and was a superintendent at the Chicago Metropolitan Mutual Assurance Company.

My parents are both HBCU graduates. My father graduated from Tuskegee Institute and my mother is a proud Aggie. They made it a point to expose my brother and me to the possibilities we could have outside the "inner city", but most importantly, within it. That we could one day be the upstanding members of the community that we looked up to. They made it a priority to frequent Black-owned businesses and professional services. Our pediatrician (Meharry), dentist (Tugaloo), and even our family pet's veterinarian (Tuskegee) were all thriving HBCU graduates. Several of my elementary school teachers, church members, and extended family were proud HBCU graduates. For me, going to college at an HBCU was never a question of if, only when.

If you ask my mother about the day I was born, she will tell you (in her dramatic storyteller fashion) that she held my tiny body close to her chest and said a prayer. "Thank you, Lord, for this child! Now, let her become an Aggie and an Alpha Mu Delta!". There is something to be said about speaking things into existence- because, last year, I celebrated twenty years in Delta Sigma Theta and, next year, I will celebrate twenty years as a graduate of NC A&T.

My mother, Marcia Wheeler (nee Britton), c/o '70, is retired from over thirty years in the Chicago Public Schools as a home economics teacher and school librarian. I had grown up hearing, and loving, all the stories about her time in Aggieland during the late 60s- the friendships she made with the other Home Ec majors in Benbow Hall; -the fried bologna sandwiches and fellowship at Boss Webster's restaurant on Market Street; -homemade ice cream served at Ward Hall; the sororities' and fraternities' evening serenades by the Holland Bowl.

Other parts that stood out were the relationships she formed with the faculty and administrators. She lovingly reminisced about the professor that taught her everything she knows about money, Dr. Katrina Porcher. When my parents dropped me off Freshman year, one of the first people in Greensboro she introduced me to was her mentor, Dr. Lucille Piggot, former Dean of Women.

Despite being born to an Aggie, I didn't become "Aggie Born" until my first time stepping on campus. In 9th grade, I went on a college tour with a local youth group. The whole tour was great, and a few schools left a lasting impression on me, but after seeing A&T with my own eyes I knew I could follow in my mother's footsteps while still forging my own path. Knowing that out-of-state student spots were limited, I applied early and was accepted.

I was bitten by the science bug in 7th grade; therefore, I knew I wanted to major in Biology in college. I did well academically in high school and always participated in extracurricular science programs. Despite feeling prepared, I had no idea what level of hard work would be required of me at NC A&T.

During the Spring semester of my Freshman year, I took, what many used to refer to as "the weed-out class", Zoology. This class inspired many to change their majors. Zoology was taught by an infamous pair of professors in the Biology department: Dr. Hill and Dr. Mitchell. They were a dynamic duo known equally for their wisecracks and knowledge. I can't remember how many times I was "roasted" for being late or unprepared for class. This class consisted of learning the taxonomic classification of organisms. The kingdoms, genus, species, etc.…for all the organisms…on Earth. This was a lot of information to be memorized and organized. Little did I know then, but this class was laying the groundwork for the thought process on which much of my graduate education would be based.

I passed Zoology, and all my other Freshman classes, but the quality of the work and the grades I was earning weren't indicative of the student I knew I could be. My parents issued the ultimatum: get more serious about your education or come back home and go to a school with fewer social distractions. I couldn't do that. I already loved A&T. So, for probably the first time, I formulated my plan for success. One distraction I identified was going back to my apartment between classes. Sometimes, I wouldn't make it back to campus on time, or I would miss class altogether. The solution I came up with was to stay on campus until my last class was finished. Most days I never left Barnes Hall. My favorite spot for studying, and people watching, was right in the main lobby. As I studied and watched people, it began to occur to me that people were also watching me study. I remember one day Dr. Hill, whose office was nearby, came and sat with me on my bench and asked me why I was sitting there every day. I told him my reasons and my plans. I wanted to be a doctor. The C's I was making were not going to get me into any graduate programs. He told me that he remembered me in his class and asked me why I didn't ask for help. I never needed help with schoolwork before, so I didn't know how to ask. Dr. Hill let me know that he and the other professors were there to help their students. He assured me that I was on the right path and that I should keep doing what I was doing. Dr. Hill would often pass by me on the way to and from his office and crack jokes, offer me snacks from the vending machine and introduce me to other faculty members in the department. This led to me being a research assistant to Dr. Bette McKnight and a teaching assistant for several classes. These types of interactions led me to learn about optometry as an option to pursue professionally.

A&T's biology department provided a strong foundation that placed me in the position that I am in today. I stand as part of the three percent of Black optometrists in the US. I have the honor each day to serve the community that I grew up in. Each day when I put on my white coat, I think about the little Black children that may come into my office that day. I am now the woman I once looked up to.

Finding my academic stride and improving my grades meant that it was time to fulfill another desire. In the spring of 2000, I was honored to pledge Delta Sigma Theta Sorority, Inc. through the Alpha Mu Chapter. Through the sisterhood of Delta, I have learned from and worked with some of the best, brightest, and most dynamic women in the country. Delta and Greek life at A&T was the icing on the cake for my Aggie experience. I am so grateful for my experiences at North Carolina A&T. The faculty that met me more than halfway and set in motion the foundation of making my goals a reality. I am blessed to have made lifelong friends that became my extended family. I am delighted to have such amazing memories. I will forever bleed blue and gold and shout Aggie Pride with the same love that I've had since day one.

About Dr. Janet Wheeler

Dr. Janet Wheeler is an optometrist in the Chicagoland area. She is the founder / clinical director of The Dry Eye Relief Center at American Vision Center, a specialty clinic focusing on the management of ocular surface diseases & ocular esthetics. Her other areas of clinical interest include nutrition, glaucoma management & myopia control.

Dr. Wheeler is passionate about providing quality care to her patients by educating them on how vision integrates into the larger picture of health & whole body wellness.

A native Chicagoan, Dr. Wheeler is proud to serve the same community she grew up in. She enjoys mentoring youth with interests in the healthcare field.

Dr. Wheeler obtained her undergraduate degree in Biology from North Carolina A&T State University in 2002 and went on to earn her Doctor of Optometry (O.D.) from the Illinois College of Optometry in 2008.

Dr. Wheeler is a life member of Delta Sigma Theta Sorority, Inc., having been initiated into the Alpha Mu Chapter in Spring 2000.

NATHAN ALEXANDER KEMP

Finding My Own Aggie Pride
Nathan Alexander Kemp

My roots run deep at North Carolina Agricultural and Technical State University. Decades before I was born the legacy and blueprint for attending this illustrious university was made. For all the years, connections, memories, and lessons learned at North Carolina A&T State University, I am forever indebted. As a third generation Aggie of the Kemp family, I am often reminded of why this university holds so strongly in my family. I often tell people that although I wasn't forced to attend A&T, it was strongly suggested and at one point I was told "either you're going to Fayetteville State University, another university that many Kemps attended, or A&T."

I count it a privilege to be a grandchild of Mr. Arthur B. Kemp, class of 1958 (Teacher's Certificate), 1965 (B.S. Industrial Arts Education) and 1977 (M.S. Industrial Arts Education), a triple Aggie. Growing up and visiting my family hometown of Raeford, NC I often heard him, my uncle and father tell stories of their time and experiences at North Carolina A&T and at the end of those conversations more often than not the question "are you going to A&T like your grandaddy?" was posed to whichever grandchild was in the room.

As I grew older I became more aware of the impact A&T made on my grandfather and the lifelong friendships he made while attending. Such as his college roommate, Mr. Van McDonald, who in his own right has left an enormous legacy at A&T. He was/is the reason tailgating during football games exists. Attending homecoming was always a highlight for me as it gave a smallish glimpse into what my future held. The uninhibited and unabashed love that radiates from alums during this week is unmatched. I can recall attending the parades sitting on my father Anthony B. Kemp, class of 1998, shoulders. Nothing but pure joy and love.

Fast-forward to 2009 and I am a senior in high school and although I planned to attend A&T I kept my options open and applied to other colleges as well. I applied to A&T in December 2009 and received my letter of acceptance in January 2010. For me, that was all I needed. I immediately responded and started preparing for the move. It's now August 2010 and I am an eager freshman excited for the journey ahead. The first night I received what I believed to be confirmation that I was in the right place in that a part of the welcome week activities was a freshman only "party" in Stallings Ballroom. Through the massive crowd of people and the darkness I bumped into a young lady I met in 2009 on a tour to UNC-Asheville, a school that I heavily considered and as it turned out, she did as well having been a native of Asheville. However, here we both are a year later after meeting for the first time bumping into each other in a massive crowd.

Nostalgia would often creep in as I would walk the campus and sit in certain classrooms because I can recall doing such with my father while he was finishing his degree. That fall I met a classmate in the cafeteria one day; I was so curious as to why she was wearing a full suit in the cafe at noon on a Tuesday. After a brief introduction she told me that she was an intern with the student government association and gave me information to apply. The next day I went to the student union, found the SGA office, and applied. The following week I found myself interviewing and eventually being selected as an intern for Mister A&T. If there was a singular moment in my life that I could reach back to and say 'this changed my life" it would be that moment. I was not sure what this new experience would bring but excited to find out.

Almost immediately I was thrown into the mix of planning, creating, and executing events and experiences. The small task of arriving at the games early to reserve seating and carry water and personal items was impactful. Eventually my work and dedication would be recognized and at the end of that year I was offered a student assistant position for the department, a biweekly paid position (second most impactful moment). Throughout the summer and into the fall I worked one on one with the new director of student government, a man I consider a mentor to this day. He gave me the opportunity and resources to work in multiple roles with different responsibilities. Those experiences opened doors of opportunity and exploration that showed me where I was supposed to be.

I am who I am because of the foundation A&T gave me. Not just my lineage but the connections and experiences I made. Like my grandfather and other family members, I ended up with great and amazing friends who inspire me daily. It has now been eleven years since we met, and I can't imagine life without them. From educators to business owners, media experts, fashion designers, economic developers and so much more, the relationships I made at A&T continue to be fruitful in my life.

At the end of my time at "T" I left with many skills and resources that would ultimately get me to the place I am now. We can often find ourselves going in one direction when an opportunity comes along and completely shifts us to a foreign land. As was my case in 2019 when I was selected to be a part of the inaugural class of fellows for the North Carolina Department of Transportation Office of HBCU Outreach graduates' program. A two-year commitment to work in any department with NCDOT. In less than a month after interviewing and accepting the position I moved from my home of Jamestown, NC to Kinston, NC for this opportunity (third most impactful moment).

My work and experience with NCDOT was a true game changer. I found myself in a position questioning where I wanted to be professionally because so many doors began to open. From working on economic development to relationship and stakeholder management, relocation projects and marinating capital improvement funds, this phase in my life brought out many of my natural talents and abilities learned by my years of work at A&T. I was able to move in and out of spaces that I hadn't been in before which led me to my current phase in life.

It has been through my professional experiences and life changes that I've grown to appreciate the true value of an Aggie education. One of my favorite quotes I learned on campus was from chancellor emeritus Dr. Lewis Dowdy "we don't teach you what to think, but how to think." While A&T gave me the knowledge base and skill development needed to find a job, it also gave me the confidence to grow and find a career path. I found a path that can guide my employment decisions for the next thirty years and connect my skills to a life path. I learned that a life path is more than your job, it is who you are in your community, family, friendship circle, and the entire world. The value proposition in a degree from North Carolina A&T State University is that you have the opportunity to find yourself, love yourself, and connect your passion to your purpose.

I am so proud to be a part of this legacy and to have influenced the next generation of Aggies in my family like my cousin Mireille L. Madison, class of 2025. I come from a long line of Aggies in my immediate family: My Grandfather, Arthur B. Kemp; Uncle, Arthur D. Kemp, PhD; Father, Anthony B. Kemp; Cousin, Desmond L. Kemp; Sister, Brooke Kemp; Cousin, Terry L. Peterkin. As well as a long list of extended family members. My Aggie Pride is not merely in being a graduate of the greatest university in the world, it is also in being a part of a living legacy that connects my immediate family to the large and dynamic network of graduates across the globe.

I will end this chapter in the Aggie Pride Compact, a proverb that was instilled in us to continue the work of excellence laid before us and to never forget:

Achieving

Great

Goals

In

Everything

Producing

Renowned

Individuals

Dedicated to

Excellence

Aggie Pride!!

There were many people who had a major impact on my life and gave me great support before, during and after college. I dedicate this chapter to my grandmothers; Jennie M. Wilson and Annie J. Kemp, and my God-Sister; Timeka S. McKoy, I will forever hold them in my heart. I would also like to dedicate this chapter to my parents; Anthony and Karen Kemp, sister; Brooke G. Kemp, brother; Anthony B. Kemp, Jr. niece; Katelyn N. Kemp, grandfather; Arthur B. Kemp, grandfather; Rudolph C. Wilson. Aunts; Cassandra Kemp, Teresa Kemp, Adriene O. Kemp-Robinson, Sherri Madison, Talya S. Wilson, and Gina Kemp. Uncles; Xavier P. Robinson, Greg Madison, Jon Wilson and Arthur D. Kemp, PhD. Cousins; Desmond L. Kemp, Ebony J. Bendida, Terry L. Peterkin, II, Austin, Anson and Arrington Kemp, Mireille and Gregory Madison, Shaniah, Talon'Dre and Tayvionna Barker, Jakai and Jakiyah Wilson, and so many more,

Thank You!

About Nathan Alexander Kemp

Nathan Alexander Kemp is a 3rd generation graduate of North Carolina Agricultural and Technical State University where he earned his Bachelor of Arts degree in History.

As a leader, educator and lifelong student, Nathan has always sought opportunities that would allow him to not only lead and showcase his talents but to engage and inspire others to do the same. It is his personal goal to uplift, empower and guide young men and women to live a better spiritual, academic, and social life. Encouraging them to keep the faith, seek wise counsel and trust that there is great purpose for their life.

Professionally, Nathan has gained experience in branding, marketing, and business development throughout his professional career. He has been afforded the opportunity to work in several industries from higher education, finance, healthcare, business, and economic development and now transportation. Nathan's occupational experience includes serving as a strategic business associate for the North Carolina Department of Transportation, Policy Liaison for Governance and planning economic development initiatives in Eastern NC with the North Carolina Global Transpark. Currently, Nathan is a Public Engagement Specialist at GoTriangle and resides in Raleigh, NC.

As a public engagement specialist Nathan's job requires community involvement and stakeholder relationships to increase access and awareness of public transportation to underrepresented communities. This is achieved by working with elected officials, nonprofit agencies, religious organizations, and educational institutions.

Nathan is co-owner of *Alexander G. Events*, a full-service event planning business in Greensboro, NC; he also operates Langston *Hurst Interior Designs*; as well as The *UncleNateSays* Podcast (formally *Nate 'n' Friends*) that focuses on politics, pop culture, religion and issues that affect the African American community.

Nathan is a certified lean six sigma green belt and a member of Phi Beta Sigma Fraternity, Inc. He is currently pursuing a master's degree in Public Administration.

Alexander G. Events

CEO/Founder: Nathan Alexander Kemp

Nathan A. Kemp, 336-706-1422

Brooke G. Kemp, 336-944-4768

alexgevents20@gmail.com

AMMEA

President: Ernest Stackhouse

ej.stackhouse@gmail.com

www.ammea.org

Allen Financial Solutions

CEO/Founder: Jay Allen

@jay83allen

@Jay Allen

allen.jonathan83@gmail.com

The Ancestor Key

CEO/Founder: Ja'el Gordon

504-356-1466

theancestor@gmail.com

The Alli Group, LLC
Real Estate Management

Founders: Lawrence & Nickia Alli

@thealligroupllc

nickia.alli@gmail.com

www.thealligroupllc.com

Ashley Little Enterprises, LLC

CEO/Founder: Dr. Ashley Little

@_ashleyalittle

@Ashley Little

aalittle08@gmail.com

www.ashleylittleenterprises.com

The Self-care Doc

CEO/Founder:

Dr. Raushannah Johnson-Verwayne
*Licensed Clinical Psychologist &
Wellness Coach*

@Ask Dr RJ

@Ask Dr RJ

www.AskDrRJ.com

**Assurance Tax & Accounting
Group, LLC**

CEO/Founder:

Kimberlee Collins-Walker

8676 Goodwood Blvd., Ste. 102

Baton Rouge, LA 70876

225-757-7518

kim@assurancetaxbr.com

www.assurancetaxbr.com

Baker & Baker Realty, LLC

CEO/Founder: Christopher Baker

@seedougieblake

@Christopher D. Baker

baker.christopher@gmail.com

The Black Techies/Podcast

CEO/Founder: Herbert L. Seward, III
*Where black culture meets the world
of technology.*

www.theblacktechies.com

BLKWOMENHUSTLE

CEO/Founder: Lashawn Dreher

@blkwomenhustle

@Blk Women Hustle

info@blkwomenhustle.com

Block Band Music & Publishing, LLC

CEO/Founder: D. Rashad Watters

919-698-2560

blockbandmusic@gmail.com

Boardroom Brand, LLC

CEO/Founder: Samuel Brown, III

@ @_gxxdy

samuel.brown.three@gmail.com

Bound By Conscious Concepts

CEO/Founder: Kathryn Lomax

@ @msklovibes223

@Klo-Kathryn Lomax

972-638-9823

klomax@bbconcepts.com

Brooks Art Collective

CEO/Founder: LaToya Brooks

@ @brooksartcollective

@brooksartcollective

brooksartcollective@gmail.com

Campaign Engineers

CEO/Founder: Chris Smith

@ @csmithatl

csmithl911@gmail.com

Chef Batts

CEO/Founder: Keith Batts

@ @chefbatts

booking@chefbatts.com

Cici's Freelance Services

CEO/Founder:

Courtney "Cici" Walker, MPA

@cicisfreelanceservices

225-288-8216

cicisfreelanceservices@gmail.com

Commit 2 Life Fitness

CEO/Founder: Joseph T. Shaw III

@commit2lifefitness

The Bitter Suite Podcast
Apple & Spotify

@thebittersuite2020

www.commit2life.com

Curves & Gangs

CEO/Founder: Patrice Murphy

@curvesandgaines

curvesandgains@gmail.com

www.curvesandgains.com

DD Jones Enterprise

CEO/Founder: Darcele Jones-Horton

darceleh@bellsouth.net

Deroune Services, LLC

CEO/Founder: Marina Zeno

337-418-0785

Eclectikread Marketing

CEO/Founder: Christa Newkirk

@chris_ta_da

info@eclectikread.com

engHERneered

CEO/Founder: Christina Caldwell, PE

engherneered@gmail.com

Enlightened Visions, Inc.

CEO/Founder: TaNisha Fordham

✉ tanisha.fordham@gmail.com

🌐 www.enlightenedvisions.org

Executive Reign

CEO/Founder: Canisha Cierra Turner

👤 @Executive Reign

☎ 804-605-6875

🌐 www.executivereign.com

🌐 www.canishacierraturner.com

February First

CEO/Founder: Cedric Livingston

Director/Writer: *February First: A Stride Towards Freedom*

🌐 www.februaryfirstmovie.com

Freeda's World Podcast

CEO/Founder: Ritha Pierre, Esq.

📷 @freedas_world

✉ accordingtorp@gmail.com

Happy Hour Investors

Co-Founder/Managing Partner:
   Jonathan Rivers

830 Glenwood Ave., Ste. 510-352

Atlanta, GA 30316

☎ 404-860-2288

✉ jonathan@hhinvestors.com

🌐 www.hhinvestors.com

Harbor Institute

CEO/Founder:
   Rasheed Ali Cromwell, J.D.

📷 @theharborinstitute

👤 @The Harbor Institute

🐦 @harborinstitute

✉ racromwell@theharborinstitute.com

HBCU 101

CEO/Founder: Jahliel Thurman

@HBCU101

jahlielthurman@gmail.com

www.hbcu101.com

HBCU Cheer Black Excellence

@HBCUcheer

HBCUcheerleaders@yahoo.com

The HBCU Band Experience with Christy Walker

CEO/Founder: Dr. Christy Walker

christywalker57@gmail.com

www.christywalker.com

The HBCU Experience Movement, LLC

CEO/Founder: Dr. Ashley Little

@_ashleyalittle

@DrAshley Little

thehbcuexperiencemovement@gmail.com

www.thehbcuexperiencemovement.com

HBCU Buzz

(HBCU Buzz | Taper, Inc. | Root Care Health)

CEO/Founder: Luke Lawal, Jr.

@lukelawal

@L & COMPANY

301-221-1719

lawal@lcompany.co

HBCU Girls Talk

CEO/Founder: TeeCee Camper

@HBCUgirlstalk

talkgirls@yahoo.com

HBCU Grad

CEO/Founder: Todd Finley

312-535-8511

www.hbcugraduates.com

HBCU Legacy Fashion

CEO/Founder: Cheylaina Fultz

@HBCULegacyFashion

@HBCULegacyFashion

contact@hbculegacyfashion.com

www.hbculegacyfashion.com

HBCU Pride Nation

CEO/Founder: Travis Jackson

@HBCUpridenation

@HBCU Pride Nation

travispjackson@gmail.com

HBCU Pulse

CEO/Founder: Randall Barnes

@HBCUpulse

@thehbcupulse

www.hbcupulse.com

HBCU Times

CEO/Founders: David Staten, Ph. &
Bridget Hollis Staten, Ph.D

@HBCU_times8892

@HBCU Times

hbcutimes@gmail.com

HBCU Wall Street

CEO/Founders:
   Torrence Reed & Jamerus Peyton

@HBCU Wall Street

info@hbcuwallstreet.com

H.E.R. Story Podcast

H.E.R. Story with J. Jamison

CEO/Founder: Janea Jamison

@herstory_podcast

#Herstorymovement

ICG Marriage & Family Therapy

CEO/Founders:

Jabari & Stephanie Walthour

@thedopesextherapist

stephanie@intimacycenterga.com

www.intimacycenterga.com

Holistic Practitioners

CEO/Founder: Tianna Bynum

@Tianna Bynum

tpb33@georgetown.edu

Johnson Capital

CEO/Founder: Marcus Johnson

@marcusdiontej

marcus@johnsoncap.com

Journee Enterprises

CEO/Founder: Fred Whit

@frederickwjr

@Fred Whit

frederickwjr@yahoo.com

J.Robins CPA, LLC
CEO/Founder: Joseph Robins
@robinscpa
@jrobinscpa
9800 Line Hwy., Ste. 261
Baton Rouge, LA 70816
225-650-7306
info@jrobinscpa.com
www.jrobinscpa.com

Kelly Collaborative Medicine
CEO/Founder: Dr. Kathyrn Kelly
10801 Lockwood Dr., Ste. 160
Silver Spring, MD 20901
301-298-1040
www.kellymedicinemd.com

The Lady BUGS
CEO/Founder: Tatiana Tinsley Dorsey
@theladybugsoffical
@HBCU Times
ladybugs_HQ@googlegroups.com

LEMM Media Group
CEO/Founder: Cremel Nakia Burney
@cremel_the_creator
cremelburney@gmail.com

Little Publishing, LLC
CEO/Founder: Dr. Ashley Little
@_ashleyalittle
@DrAshley Little
info@ashleyalittle.com
www.ashleylittleenterprises.com

Swing Into Their Dreams Foundation
Co-Founders: Pamela Parker and
  Lynn Demmons
swingintotheirdreams@gmail.com
www.swingintotheirdreams.com

LK Productions

CEO/Founder: Larry King

@lk_rrproduction

@Larry King

lkproduction@yahoo.com

The Marching Podcast

CEO/Founder: Joseph Beard

marchingpodcast@gmail.com

www.themarchingpodcast.com

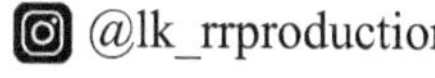

Lynch Law, PLLC

CEO/Founder: Chance D. Lynch, Esq.

1015A Roanoke Ave., Ste. A

Roanoke Rapids, NC 27870

252-535-1251

Marching Sport

CEO/Founder: Gerard Howard

gerardhoward@gmail.com

The Marching Force

700 Emancipation Dr.

Hampton, VA 23668

www.supportthematchingforce.com

McKallen Medical

CEO/Founder: Sade Stephenson,
MSN, RN, AGACNP-BC

9253 Hermosa Ave., Ste. B

Rancho Cucamonga, CA 91730

747-225-6776

mckallenmedical@gmail.com

www.mckallenmedicaltraining.com

Minority Cannabis Business Association

President: Shanita Penny

[Instagram] @Minority Cannabis

[Facebook] @MCBA.Org

[Twitter] @MinCannBusAssoc

[LinkedIn] @Minority Cannabis Business Association

[Phone] 202-681-2889

[Email] info@minoritycannabis.org

[Web] www.minoritycannabis.org

Mills Academy

CEO/Founder: Airneica Mills

[Phone] 662-822-6976

[Email] millsacademy1@gmail.com

MilRo Entertainment

CEO/Founder: Chevis Anderson

[Email] milrosplace@yahoo.com

NC Dance District

CEO/Founder: Dr. Kellye Worth Hall

[Instagram] @divadoc5

[Facebook] @Kellye Worth Hall

[Email] delta906@gmail.com

Never2Fly2Pray

CEO/Founder: Jeffrey Lee Sawyer

[Instagram] @never2fly2pray

[Facebook] @Jeffrey Lee

[Email] htdogwtr@yahoo.com

NXLevel Travel (NXLTRVL)

CEO: Hercules Conway

@herc3k

@Hercules Conway

COO: Newton Dennis

@nxlevel

@Newton Dennis

info@nxleveltravel.com

www.nxleveltravel.com

The Phoenix Professional Network

CEO/Founder: DJavon Alston

@thephoenixnetwork757

@DJavon Alston

thephoenixnetwork757@gmail.com

OEDM Group

CEO/Principal Owner: Justin Blake

@oedmgroup.com

contact@oedmgroup.com

www.oedmgroup.com

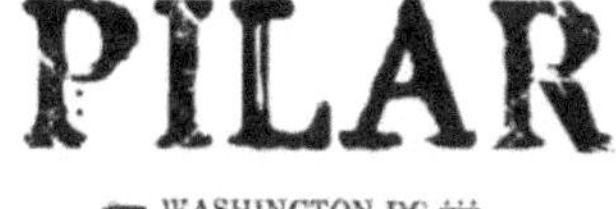

PILAR

Co-Owner: Nate Perry

@barpilar

nate@pilardc.com

PacketStealer Gaming

CEO/Founder: David Matthews

packetstealer@outlook.com

Queen Series

CEO/Founder: Randall Barnes

aqueenseries@gmail.com

Reid Creative Solutions, LLC

CEO/Founder: Aja Reid

919-822-2892

info@reidcreativesolutions.com

www.reidcreativesolutions.com

Shani L., Relationship Enthusiast

CEO/Founder: Porscha Lee Taylor

@shanilrelationshipenthusiast

info@shanilfarmer.com

www.shanilfarmer.com

SayYes

Say Yes, LLC

CEO/Founder: Porscha Lee Taylor

@sayyesplanners

info@sayyescareer.com

www.sayyesplanners.com

She Is Magazine

CEO/Founder: Ciara Horton

@sheisemagazine

@Ciara Horton

ciarasheisemagazine.com

SC DJ WORM 803

CEO/Founder: Jamie Brunson

@SCDJWORM803

@SC DJ Worm 803

@SCDJWORM803

@SC DJ Worm 803

scdjworm803@gmail.com

www.scdjworm803.com

Southern University A&M College

801 Harding Blvd.

Baton Rouge, LA 70807

225-771-4500

Southern University Alumni Federation

124 Roosevelt Steptoe Dr.

Baton Rouge, LA 70807

225-771-4200

sualumni@sualumni.org

Springbreak Watches (SPGBK)

CEO/Founder: Kwame Molden

@SPGBK

@Kwame Molden

info@springbreakwatches.com

Stamp'd Travel

CEO/Founder:

Jocelyn Hadrick Alexander

@jocehadyou

jocelyn.h.alexander@gmail.com

www.stampdtravel.com

Success and Religion

CEO/Founder: Micheal Taylor

successismyreligion@gmail.com

Sugar Top Spirit & Beverage Co.

CEO/Founder: Terri White

@sugartopspirits

@sugartopspirits

tl.white412@gmail.com

www.sugartopspirits.com

SwagHer

Vice President of Sales / Marketing:

Jarmel Roberson

@swaghermagazine

jroberson@swagher.net

www.swagher.net

TLW Photography
CEO/Founder: Taylor Whitehead
✉ mrknowitall91@aol.com

The Urban Learning & Leadership Center, Inc.
President/Co-Founder:
John W. Hodge, Ed.D
✉ jhodge@ulleschools.com

Uplift Clothing Apparel
CEO/Founder: Jermaine Simpson
⊡ @upliftclothingapparel
🌐 www.upliftclothingapparel.com

The Vernon Group Cooperative Solutions
CEO/Founder: Anthony V. Stevens
⊡ @investednu
✉ info@vernongroupllc.com

Upward Path
CEO/Founder:
Cameron Chamlers Dupree
⊡ @upwardpathtc
✉ contact@upwardpathtc.com
🌐 www.upwardpathtc.com

Vision Tree, LLC
CEO/Founder: Dr. Jorim Reed
⊡ @upwardpathtc
✉ visiontreellc@gmail.com

VJR Real Estate

CEO/Founder: Victor Collins, Jr.

@vjrtherealtor

vic@thevjrgroup.com

Yard Talk 101

CEO/Founder: Jahliel Thurman

@YardTalk101

www.yardtalk101.com

We Are Educated, Inc.

We Are Educated, Inc.

CEO/Founder: Ayanna Spivey

@ayannaceleste

ayanna.spivey@yahoo.com

Zoom Technologies, LLC

CEO/Founder: Torrence Reed

@torrencereed3

support@zoom-technologies.co

Yard Stubs

CEO/Founder: Cremel Burney

@YardStubs

partnerships@yardstubs.com

www.yardstubs.com